HEALTH , WEALTH AND PLEASURE
in Colorado and New Mexico

A CENTENNIAL EDITION

Museum of New Mexico Press
SANTA FE

CENTENNIAL
EDITION
COPYRIGHT
© 1980

MUSEUM OF ▦ NEW MEXICO
PRESS
P.O. Box 2087, Santa Fe, New Mexico 87503
ISBN 0-89013-126-0

Library of Congress Catalog Card No. 80-82428

FOREWORD

The quaint and fascinating little volume reproduced here — an exceedingly rare, and quite unusual find — is from among the superb collections of the Museum of New Mexico. This antique imprint, the earliest forerunner of a multitude of publications in similar vein, was issued by the (predecessors of today's) Denver and Rio Grande Western Railroad. From its inception in October, 1870, that venerable Rocky Mountain transportation institution has exhibited not only an amazing will to survive, but considerable adeptness in advertising its wares.

Beset during the very first decade of its existence by every difficulty — economic, social, physical and financial, with control of its operations, its traffic, its very life, placed unwillingly in the hands of a powerful rival — the Denver and Rio Grande won through. Early in 1880, upon regaining possession of its property, then comprising only 337 miles of three-foot gauge track south from Denver, the railroad entered upon a tremendous campaign of extension and expansion. Less than three years later, at the end of 1882, 945 miles of additional route through the mountains of Colorado and New Mexico had been surveyed, grades excavated and smoothed, uncounted bridges erected, hand-hewn ties bedded in the native earth, and rails spiked in place.

By the end of the following year, in conjunction with an associated company in Utah, the system totalled 1,685 miles of narrow-gauge railroad, including a main line 772 miles long between Denver and Ogden. Feeder branch lines reached into a great many of the frontier agricultural and mining areas of southern and western Colorado, northern New Mexico, and eastern Utah.

Such an enterprise was indeed worthy of exploitation by word and illustration, and to the task came the legendary Major Shadrach K. Hooper. Entering the service of the Rio Grande as general passenger and ticket agent in June, 1884, he is generally perceived as being the initial prime mover in the railroad's advertising. Credited not only with originating the memorable slogan, "Scenic Line of the World," Major Hooper also devised the romantic "Currecanti Needle" herald used as the trademark which graced the railroad's publicity and literature for very near a half century.

Less well recognized in modern times, however, is the Denver and Rio Grande's prolific dispersion, worldwide, of numerous pamphlets of the kind now before you. Frequent editions, often on an annual basis, of such titles as *Rhymes of the Rockies, or What the Poets Have Found to Say of the Beautiful Scenery on the Denver and Rio Grande* (1887); *Tourist's Handbook* (1887 — 25,000 copies each year); *Valleys of the Great Salt Lake* (1890); *The Judge and the Colonel* (1895); *The Gold Fields of Colorado* (1896); *Fertile Lands of Colorado* (1899); *Sights, Places and Resorts in the Rockies* (1900); *With Nature in Colorado* (1901); *Camping in the Rockies* (1903); *Ancient Ruins of the Southwest* (1909); and the now much sought after *Around the Circle* (1896) exemplify the remarkable diversity of subjects — as well as the inventive titles endowed by the fertile imagination of Shadrach Hooper.

But here, in the reader's hands, we behold the forerunner of them all: *Health, Wealth and Pleasure in Colorado and New Mexico*, copyrighted 1881 by F. C. Nims who, in the period June 1880 through May 1884, preceded Major Hooper as general passenger agent of the Denver and Rio Grande and established a public relations custom which survived well beyond the turn of the century. How fortunate it is that the Museum of New Mexico Press has decided to revive this ancient little gem from among its treasures and, nearly a century later, make it available to the public once again.

Jackson Thode
Denver, Colorado
December, 1978

HEALTH, WEALTH AND PLEASURE
in Colorado and New Mexico

GRAND CAÑON OF THE ARKANSAS.

(Frontispiece)

HEALTH, WEALTH AND PLEASURE

IN

Colorado and New Mexico.

A RELIABLE TREATISE

ON THE

FAMOUS PLEASURE AND HEALTH RESORTS, AND THE RICH MINING AND AGRICULTURAL REGIONS

OF THE

ROCKY MOUNTAINS.

"Oh! there is sweetness in the mountain air,
And Life, that bloated ease can never hope to share."
— *Byron.*

ILLUSTRATED.

CHICAGO:
BELFORD, CLARKE & CO., PUBLISHERS.
1881.

CONTENTS

CONTENTS.

LIST OF ILLUSTRATIONS

MONUMENT PARK.

INTRODUCTION.

THE Denver and Rio Grande Railway was commenced in 1870, a few months only after the Kansas Pacific Railway had crossed the plains and reached the foot of the Rocky Mountains at Denver. The object of its projectors was to construct a railway along the eastern base of the back-bone of the continent, and then to pierce the mountains by branches to reach the mining districts whenever and wherever they proved to be suffi-ciently productive. With this definite purpose in view a three-foot gauge was chosen, which ten years' experience has proved to be eminently adapted to meet the requirements of the country. The mountain-base line was gradually constructed due south from Denver to El Moro, two hundred and six miles. The first mining branch was that to the coal fields near Cañon City, which preceded by one year the completion of the road to the coal fields at El Moro. Then followed the extension over Veta Pass, head-ing toward the silver mines of the San Juan country. Next came the extension to Leadville, which was delayed for a year by a bitter legal con-test with a rival road for possession of the Grand Cañon of the Arkansas. No sooner was Leadville reached than the extraordinary mining activ-ity developed throughout the mountains of Colorado, which has placed this state foremost in the production of precious metals, justified the un-precedented feat of carrying on the construction of no less than seven extensions at once. In the effort to reach the spots where nature hides her treasures the greatest engineering difficulties yet encountered on this con-tinent have been overcome, the deepest gorges have been traversed, the loftiest ranges have been climbed. In five different places the summit of the Continental Divide has been crossed, and the " Pioneer Line " on these extensions is following the course of streams whose waters lead to the Pacific.

By way of introduction we will briefly enumerate the characteristic features of interest to the traveler on the different divisions of this rail-way, which is justly termed " The Scenic Line of America." It skirts along the western edge of the Great Plains, the vast and sublime treeless expanse that hardly a score of years since was known as the Great Amer-ican Desert, for over two hundred miles, at just the proper distance to show in all their majesty and sublimity two of the loftiest snow-clad ranges of the Rocky Mountain system. From Denver to La Veta, a dis-tance of one hundred and ninety-one miles, the panorama of mountain and plain seen from its cars has no equal, as regards extent of vision, on the North American continent. To the traveler from the eastern sections of the Union it seems to open a new heavens and a new earth. Accustomed to the limited horizon of the east, with wonder and delight he finds his vision ranging over spaces vaster than he had ever dreamed could be compassed by human sight. From beholding mountains a hundred miles to the north, he turns to see other mountains a hundred miles to the south. To the east, the plains, solitary and untrammeled as the ocean, rise up to meet the sky. Lying in depressions of the plains, like parts of a mosaic, are rapid mountain streams, along whose narrow, fertile valleys are beautiful cities, neat villages, and attractive farms, over whose surfaces flow the tiny crystal rills from the irrigating ditches, without which even the hardiest shrubs would wither and die. Vision is assisted by the wonderful transparency of the atmosphere, and objects many miles distant appear near at hand, while even the farthest mountain peaks lie clear-cut and distinct against the sky.

Bayard Taylor has said that nowhere along the entire extent of the Alps is there a point from which they can be seen to so good advantage as the Rocky Mountains are beheld from Denver. Hence there could be no more fitting starting point for what is essentially a Rocky Mountain railway.

In Denver we find a city of scarcely more than ten years' growth (for in 1870 it was still only a collection of wooden shanties) planted on an arid plain, a thousand miles removed from any large manufacturing center, yet containing all the appliances and most of the luxuries of our modern civilization. The telegraph, telephone, electric light, steam heating works, gas, and other modern inventions, which a population of 40,000 people have found it necessary to employ, extend to the hotels, private houses, depots, stores, etc. The markets are excellent, and not only gather fresh produce from every State, but reach out to every quarter of the globe for the choicest viands that can tempt the palate of the somewhat extravagant purchasers. The livery establishments furnish fast steppers that would elsewhere hardly be looked for outside the race-course. There are shops filled with Rocky Mountain specimens, including both the mineral and animal productions. The mineralogist and man of science will find at Argo the most complete reduction works of its kind in America.

But to return to the railway. Fifty-two miles southward from Denver the summit of the watershed which separates the valleys of the Arkansas and the Platte is crossed. Here is a lakelet, the shore of which the train skirts for half a mile. Then it glides down the Valley of the Monument, and twenty-three miles further arrives at Colorado Springs, from which point a branch line, five miles long, leads to Manitou.

Forty-five miles southward we come to Pueblo, where the chief objects of interest are the Peublo Smelting and Refining Works, and the iron furnace and steel works of the Colorado Coal and Iron Company.

Delightful as the scenery is from Denver to Pueblo, it is merely an introduction to the greater wonders that are unfolded when the Railway penetrates into the fastnesses of the mountains, and lays bare the very "heart of the Rockies." Half a score of branches, varying in length from five to three hundred miles, penetrate the famous mining regions of Colorado, in most of which they are the pioneer and only rail line — the enthusiastically welcome l herald of civilization, trade, and progress. Of the eight hundred miles of road now operated, in fact of the entire twelve hundred that will be completed before the end of the current year, it can safely be said that there is scarcely a mile of tame scenery. Everywhere the attention is held by the shifting phases of the mountain view, near or distant, the beauty of the extensive parks, or the picturesque grandeur of the cañons and mountain passes. The scenery changes with every mile.

At Denver, Long's Peak is seen rearing its majestic proportions against the northern sky; westward Mounts Rosalie and Evans rise grandly above the other peaks of the snowy range, and Gray's Peak and James' Peak peer out from among their gigantic brethren, above the pine-clad foothills, while Pike's Peak, the mighty landmark that guided the gold-hunters of '59, in plain view from Denver, rises apace till the traveler sees it abreast of him at Colorado Springs, towering above that city and Manitou.

Diverging from Pueblo, one hundred and twenty miles south of Denver, the railway enters the mountains by three avenues: through the majestic gateways of Veta Pass, Grape Creek Cañon, and the Grand Cañon of the Arkansas. One mile above Cañon City it dives into a cleft in the granite rock and, passing through an awful gorge three thousand feet in depth, emerges above it into the upper Arkansas valley, where the constant succession of beautiful and varied scenery, mountains and cañons, parks and pleasant valleys, are a constant wonder and delight as the train skirts the roaring torrent of the Arkansas, which dashes headlong eastward toward the plains.

At South Arkansas, fifty-six miles from Cañon City, the line for Poncho Springs, the Monarch mines, and the Gunnison, diverges to the southwest, and at Nathrop, eighteen miles farther, the branch to Alpine runs westward into the mountains. About fourteen miles from Leadville the station for the Twin Lakes, four miles distant, is reached.

Leadville is situated in old California Gulch, four miles east of the Arkansas river. We call it *old*, because it is so relatively, having been the scene of one of the earliest and most successful gold excitements in the history of Colorado Territory. It is estimated that this gulch has yielded over twelve million dollars from its gold washings, and it is reported that the gold seekers of early times were quite familiar with what they termed the "heavy sand," which they, however, failed to recognize as the now celebrated "soft carbonates."

At the mouth of this gulch stands Malta, the older town, although now known only as a suburb of Leadville. Here the road again diverges, one branch passing Leadville and crossing the Continental Divide at Fremont Pass, the highest point yet reached by any railway in North America, 11,540 feet above the level of the sea, to Robinson, Kokomo, and beyond. At Fremont Pass the track reaches the very verge of timber line, surrounded by bare and forbidding peaks that hold during the hottest summer the snow and frosts of winter. Amid these awful and lonely surroundings is the wonderful curve around the tiny springs that are the headwaters of the Arkansas river. From the storm-swept summit the traveler views, with rapt surprise, the Mountain of the Holy Cross, bearing aloft its mystic symbol in tracks of virgin snow. The western branch continues straight up the Arkansas valley from Malta, crosses the continental watershed at Tennessee Pass, penetrates the mining districts of Eagle river, and the romantic scenery at the foot of the Mountain of the Holy Cross.

Immediately west of the huge mountain barrier which forms so grand a feature in the landscape to the left of the railway, all the way from the cañon of the Arkansas to Leadville, lies the Gunnison country. For a distance of two hundred miles the great Sangre de Cristo range has but one well-marked depression, and that occurs opposite the mouth of the South Arkansas, whose stream is fed by tributaries taking their sources in and about the depression. Through the gap, Poncho Pass, to the southward, leads into the San Luis valley, in the drainage of the Rio Grande; Marshall Pass, deviating to the westward, leads to the valley of the Tomichi, a main tributary of Gunnison river. The streams which flow southeastward down Poncho and Marshall Passes unite with the South Arkansas near Poncho Springs.

The Gunnison division of the railway starts from a point near the mouth of the South Arkansas river, follows that stream to Poncho Springs, sends off a branch to Maysville and other mining towns near by, and then crosses Marshall Pass, and so down the Tomichi to Gunnison City, situated on the stream from which it takes its name. From Gunnison City most of the chief mining districts of this great division of Colorado will be reached by branches running up the tributary streams which spread out like a fan from Gunnison City as a center.

One mile above Cañon City, and just at the entrance of the Grand Cañon, the Wet Mountain Valley branch leaves the main line, and, following up Grape Creek in a southwest direction for thirty-two miles, through a cañon of wonderful beauty, terminates at Westcliffe, from which point the mines of Silver Cliff, Rosita, and Bassick, numerous stamp-mills in the vicinity, and a large agricultural population are supplied. The agricultural importance of the Wet Mountain Valley, and its scenic beauty, will be found fully described in their proper place.

Returning to Pueblo we now follow the railway southward and westward. From Pueblo to Cuchara, a distance of fifty miles, the line has few attractions beyond the ever-varying features of the Spanish Peaks viewed from the cars as the train describes a tortuous course across the drainage of the country. At Cuchara the line branches. The El Moro division makes straight for Fisher's Peak, the most prominent headland of the Raton Mountains, but fails to arrive at its destination, for five miles beyond El Moro it runs to ground in the enormous coal veins which flank the mountain. At El Moro the entire coke supply of Colorado is manufactured. Over 26,000 tons of coke were shipped from this point during 1880, and supplied sixty-one out of the sixty-eight furnaces in the State. A very striking view is to be seen nightly from El Moro. It is a semicircle of two hundred coke ovens all aglow, backed by the dark, basaltic columns of the Raton range.

The line from Cuchara westward ascends the fertile and picturesque Cuchara Valley for twenty-two miles, and then climbs up Veta Pass, rising by short curves•and steep grades into the very realms of cloud-land, nearly two miles above sea level, affording magnificent and far-reaching views of the Spanish Peaks, Veta Mountain, and the romantic valley between. Thence the railway traverses the great inland basin of the San Luis Valley, striking the Rio Grande two hundred and fifty miles from Denver and one hundred and thirty from Pueblo, at Alamosa. From Alamosa the line runs almost due south twenty-nine miles, leaving the river ten miles to the eastward, to the Mexican settlement of Antonito, where it again forks.

From this point the traveler may be prepared for entering a new world — whether he goes south, to find himself among the still living remains of Montezuma on the tributaries of the Rio Grande, or hastening along the edge of the stupendous Toltic Gorge, over the dizzy heights of the Chama summit, on through the dense forests of the Tierra Amarilla, reaches the great San Juan country, a land so entirely unlike in verdure, in climate and in scenery anything to which he is accustomed in the Rocky Mountains, north and east, that he can scarcely believe himself still in Colorado.

Born of the new era — the railroad era to the San Juan country—is the now famous town of Durango, already the metropolis of southwestern Colorado. The road is under contract to be completed to this point by June 1, and to Silverton, forty-five miles north, two or three months later.

The New Mexico division extends from Antonito, ninety miles south, to Espanola, New Mexico, twenty-three miles from Santa Fé, which gap is bridged by an excellent line of six-horse coaches. Climbing the mesas at the foot of San Antonio Mountain, the railway passes over an elevated country, underlaid with volcanic rock, and covered with park-like forests of piñons (*pinos edalis*), the edible nut-bearing pine of the Rocky Mountains. The cones which contain the seeds mature about once in three years, at which periods all the denizens of the forests, the deer, coneys, bears, squirrels and wild turkeys, prairie dogs, grow fat. The nuts are delicious eating, and are frequently sold as an article of commerce. Sixty-four miles south of Antonito, at Barranca Station, is the place of divergence for the celebrated Ojo Caliente hot springs, twelve miles distant by stage.

Just below Barranca the railway makes a rapid descent of some 1,200 feet in seven miles, through the Comanche Cañon, and reaches the banks of the Rio Grande at Embudo. For several miles below this point the large, black, basaltic boulders, which lie in great profusion to the west of the track, are many of them covered with Indian hieroglyphics which can plainly be seen from the car windows.

PRAIRIE DOGS.

A short distance from Embudo we enter the populous portions of the Rio Grande Valley, where the banks of the river on both sides are thickly studded with Indian pueblos and Mexican plazas. Twenty miles above Embudo, on an eastern tributary of the Rio Grande, is situated the Pueblo de Taos, the most interesting of all the Indian fortifications, in which the native population still live the primitive life of times long past. Nor is the end of the road, called Espanola, by any means devoid of interest. The fine plaza of Santa Cruz lies directly opposite, on the east side of the Rio Grande, with its rudely ornate church. About a mile immediately below the depot is the Indian pueblo of San Juan. In the high bluffs opposite the pueblo, as well as in many other places in this region, are to be found the remains of cliff dwellings, which have very naturally attracted much interest.

The most attractive features of the old Mexican city of Santa Fé, capital of the Territory of New Mexico, are fully presented hereafter.

Such is a general outline of the Denver and Rio Grande Railway, and certainly no other road can offer so many and so varied attractions to the tourist. In and around all the mountain passes are snow-fed streams, and beautiful lakelets filled with mountain trout. In the secluded cañons are the lurking places of the cinnamon bear and mountain lion; and among the loftiest crags the feeding places of the mountain sheep.

If the health-seeker requires more than pure air and grand scenery, the railway takes him to the famed effervescent soda and iron springs of Manitou, the hot mineral springs of Cañon City, Ojo Caliente, Pagosa, Poncho, and Cottonwood, the soda springs of Leadville, and many others less known but equally valuable.

In addition to its local attractions the Denver and Rio Grande Railway, in connection with the Atchison, Topeka and Santa Fé Railroad, is by far the pleasantest through line between the Missouri river and Denver, passing on the latter for four hundred miles along the beautiful Arkansas Valley, and on the former one hundred and twenty miles, parallel with the grand mountain ranges before described.

Throughout the mountains, in close proximity to the railway, there are hundreds of parks, valleys and cañons, in which pleasure-seekers may find secluded camping places, hunt and fish as long as they please, and even, if they wish, so hide themselves that they shall hardly see a human face during the summer. In the vastness of the mountains "the elbow room" that they afford, in which to escape for a time from the fierce struggles and intense mental strain of modern civilization, lies their chief attraction to many travelers.

For people from the East who seek health through a change of climate and associations, the country traversed by the Denver and Rio Grande Railway offers inducements that are nowhere surpassed. The pure, dry air of the plains and mountains, rarefied by an elevation of from one to two miles above the sea, and often in a high degree electrical, is bracing and exhilarating to the lungs. For asthma it is an almost unfailing specific, as hundreds of persons, confirmed asthmatics before coming to Colorado, but here able to breathe with comfort, and in the enjoyment of health, will make haste to testify. Those who have weak lungs, or who are in the incipient stages of consumption, seldom fail of relief in this climate, especially if they live out of doors as much as possible, and are not afraid of the sunshine, which is one of the crowning glories of Colorado. Nowhere in America are so many fine days. During some seasons a cloudy day is almost as rare as an eclipse, and there can be no doubt that cheerfulness and bodily and mental activity are promoted by the absence of dark days, fogs, mists and dampness. If, as Longfellow sings,

"Some days must be dark and dreary,"

in this climate they are reduced to the minimum, and during some years happily missed from the calendar altogether.

While its scenic attractions and advantages of climate will always conspire to make the Denver and Rio Grande Railway popular with tourists and health-seekers, its existence is principally due to facts of another nature. The millions of dollars expended in its construction have been furnished by capitalists for the purpose of opening highways to the rich mineral deposits of Colorado, now the leading bullion producing State of the Union. The phenomenal rapidity with which it pushes forward half a score or more of extensions at the same time, through tortuous cañons where frequently the surveyors who locate the line have to be let down over precipices by ropes, and over rugged mountain passes, higher than any railways in the world except some in South America, overcoming obstacles which a few years ago would have been considered insurmountable, has its explanation in the wonderful development of mineral production which has been witnessed in Colorado during the past three years, and the many valuable discoveries that are constantly being made in the districts into which it penetrates. Let us consider the record of three years. In 1878 the entire bullion production of the State, including copper and lead, was about $8,000,000; in 1879 it was $16,000,000; in 1880 it was $24,000,000. No one acquainted with the present condition of the mines estimates the probable bullion product of 1881 at less than from $30,000,000 to $32,000,-000, while many place it much higher. Those best informed in regard to the mines assert that mining in Colorado is yet in its infancy, and that there will be abundant opportunity for prospectors for a hundred years and more. There are large areas that have hardly been prospected at all, and others that have been but superficially skimmed over; while even in the oldest districts new lodes are continually being discovered, and forsaken ones developed into paying mines. During the entire history of mining for the precious metals in America, it is doubtful if any section has ever afforded better opportunities for acquiring wealth by legitimate mining operations than are offered by Colorado to-day. The railway takes you at once to the center of the richest mining districts, transports supplies and mining machinery at cheap rates, and in return carries ore and bullion to the different competing markets.

DENVER TO PUEBLO.

THE line of the Denver and Rio Grande Railway from Denver to Lead-ville, known as the First Division, is two hundred and seventy-nine miles in length. From Denver to Pueblo, one hundred and twenty miles, it takes a southerly course, crossing the divide, or table-land, which separates the Platte and the Arkansas rivers, and striking the latter at Pueblo. From Pueblo to Leadville it follows the course of the Arkansas west and north, thus reaching Leadville without crossing either of the mountain ranges, a fact of much importance in winter, when the mountain passes are frequently obstructed with snow.

DENVER.

The city of Denver lies, at an altitude of 5,197 feet, near the western border of the plains, within twelve miles of the Rocky Mountains, the Colorado or front range of which may be seen for an extent of over two hundred miles, forming a magnificent feature of the extended landscape. The plains encompass the city, stretching for hundreds of miles to the north, east, and south, and westward to the mountains. Reaching Denver from the east, after traveling for hundreds of miles over the bare and lonely plains, the sensation is not unlike first stepping on land after a voy-age at sea. The contrast is delightful between the great rolling, verdure-less tract, whose magnitude can hardly be realized by those who have never crossed it, and the beautiful city which the traveler comes upon suddenly, lying in a slight depression, embowered in thick-set shade trees. Denver is well entitled to the appellation " the Queen City of the Plains," by which its citizens delight to designate it.

The city was born of the first Pike's Peak gold excitement in 1858-9. In 1860 it was a straggling camp consisting principally of log cabins and tents in about equal proportions; in 1870 the United States census showed a population of 4,579; and the last census, June 1, 1880, enumerated 35,719 inhabitants. Since that date over 600 buildings have been erected, and the population has increased to over 40,000. The annual directory for 1881 shows a gain of 6,043 names over the year previous, and the publish-ers, with accustomed liberality, place the number of inhabitants at 50,000. An examination of the census returns, and a glance at Denver's building improvements since 1876, will show that no city in the Union is having a more rapid and substantial growth.

The principal business streets are Blake, Holladay, Larimer, Lawrence, Fifteenth, and Sixteenth; but business is by no means confined to these, being scattered over a large area. There are four national and two state banks, the aggregate deposits of which, October 1, 1880, were $6,123,358.86. The amount of eastern exchange drawn during 1880 was $65,000,000. There are two home fire insurance companies, one live-stock insurance company, and three co-operative life insurance associations. The water supply is taken from the Platte river above the city, and conveyed to a large reservoir, known as Lake Archer, from which it is distributed by the Holly system. Gas was introduced several years ago, and the Denver Gas Company have extended their pipes to nearly all parts of the city; but during the present year it will be superseded, as a means of lighting the streets, by the Brush electric light. The Denver Steam Heating Company have over two miles of pipes laid. The telephone is in general use, and the large poles that support its numerous wires add to the metropolitan appearance of the streets. A branch of the United States mint is located here, but is used only for assays, and not for coinage. Denver is the capital of Colorado, and contains the state offices and the United States courts for the District of Colorado. It is also the county-seat of Arapahoe county, a fine court-house for which is now in process of erection at a cost of $250,000.

COLORADO COLLEGE.

The public schools of Denver are free to all residents, and are regarded as among the best in the country. The course of study at the high school is quite as extensive and thorough as that of the best schools of similar character in the East. The school buildings are all substantial structures of brick or stone, conveniently arranged in modern style. Aside from the public schools there are several important educational institutions, the most prominent of which are the University of Denver, and Colorado Seminary, under the control of the Methodist Episcopal church, recently inaugurated in a fine building erected in 1880; Jarvis Hall, boarding and day school for boys, and Wolfe Hall Seminary for young ladies, managed by the Episcopal church; Brinker Collegiate Institute, Colorado Business College, and St. Mary's Academy, a large Roman Catholic institution.

The Windsor hotel is a large and handsome structure, 125 × 200 feet in size, ground measurement, and five stories and basement in height. The two façades are of a beautiful pink-tinted Colorado stone. It was opened in 1880, and is furnished and kept in first-class style, taking rank with the best hotels in the country. Its location is but four blocks from the Union depot, at the corner of Larimer and Eighteenth. streets, convenient to the business center of the city. The Tabor opera house, begun last year and to be completed this summer, has a frontage of 125 feet on Sixteenth street and 225 on Curtis street. The exterior will be of iron and Colorado pressed brick, with Manitou stone trimmings. The auditorium is designed to accommodate 1,600 persons, and will be fitted up in a style equal to that of the best eastern theaters. The Tabor block, corner of Sixteenth and Larimer streets, was completed in 1880 at a cost of $225,000. It is built of Ohio sandstone, and from its lofty height and architectural beauty is one of the most noticeable buildings in the city. In addition to these the Glenarm hotel, now used as a state-house, the King block, the new Episcopal Cathedral of St. John's, the Central Presbyterian church, and many other important buildings are evidences of the solid character of Denver's remarkable growth. The number of beautiful and costly private residences is in keeping with the character of its business blocks. Fourteenth street and Capital Hill, an eminence in the southeastern part of the city, are the sites of many tasteful and expensive dwellings. Hotel and boarding-house accommodations are ample and of superior quality, and the rates but little higher than in seaboard cities.

The works of the Boston and Colorado Smelting Company, at Argo, in the suburbs of Denver, are among the finest and most extensive gold and silver reducing establishments in the world. The buildings are of immense size, and are constructed of cut stone, with corrugated iron roofs. The large ore house alone is 450 feet long by 120 feet wide, and the principal smelting furnaces occupy another building nearly 300 feet in length; beside which there are the refining works, offices, and other large buildings. No expense is spared, either in chemical and practical experiments or machinery, to enable the company to treat all classes of ore, including the most refractory, and their success has been a marked factor in the mining development of Colorado. Their shipments of gold, silver and copper in 1879 were $2,449,500, and in 1880 they were $2,730,500. To produce these results there are thirty great kilns for roasting and desulphurizing the ore, and requiring wood for fuel; ten ore calciners, or roasting furnaces; eight calcining furnaces in the refining department, and five melting furnaces. Each of the thirty large furnaces has a smokestack 100 feet high. The consumption of coal reaches one hundred tons per day, this being a species of consumption for which the climate of Colorado is not an antidote.

The Colorado Coal and Iron Company has a rolling-mill situated on the south side of the Platte, opposite the Boston and Colorado Smelting Works. The mill is adapted for making all ordinary sizes of iron rail and merchant iron; and it is proposed to erect puddling furnaces here to work pig iron from the company's furnaces at South Pueblo, and to put in machinery for the manufacture of railway splice bars, spikes, bolts, etc.

The Union Depot, used by the Denver and Rio Grande Railway and the Union Pacific Lines, is a beautiful stone structure, £03 feet long and 63 feet wide, with a French roof, and tower 165 feet high. It is two stories in height, the upper floor being used for railway offices and a hotel. On the first floor, conveniently located, are the baggage room, 62 × 75 feet; ladies' waiting room, 56 × 59 feet; gents' waiting room, 60 × 62 feet; dining room, 44 × 62 feet; two express rooms, each 30 × 62, with fire and burglar proof vaults; mail rooms, telegraph and ticket offices, barber shop, lunch and check stands, fitted with all modern improvements for the convenience and comfort of the traveling public. The freight depot of the Denver and Rio Grande Railway, between Tenth and Eleventh streets, is a large, handsome stone building.

The car and repair shops of the Denver and Rio Grande Railway, in the south part of the city, constitute the largest manufacturing establishment in Denver. Over 550 workmen are constantly employed, and it is frequently necessary to greatly increase this force. All repairs of locomotives and rolling-stock are made here, and both freight and passenger cars are manufactured, although the former have been in such demand that but few coaches could be built. The present capacity of the works is about five new cars a day, but with the completion of the car shops now building it will be easy to turn out double that number. The buildings are all of brick, with corrugated iron roofs, and are exceptionally high, well lighted, roomy and convenient. The office, which fronts the main track, is 35 × 60 feet in size, two stories high, with large windows, making it a model office building. Back of it is the store-room, having the appearance of an extensive hardware store, 208 × 57 feet in size, with a high roof. Under it is a basement of equal size. Next is the machine shop, 290 × 75 feet, with a truss-roof that does away with the use of columns. Surmounting the roof is a skylight 26 feet wide and 280 feet long. Adjoining are the engine and boiler rooms, both models of neatness and convenience, a tool room and brass room, 60 × 28 feet, and a tin shop of similar size. The smoke-stack, 107 feet high, is built square at the bottom, but rises in octagonal form, with panels. The car shops, now building, comprise a machine department, 260 × 60 feet, and an erecting department, 240 × 60, with a second story of the same proportions, which will be used for cabinet work. The dimensions of the paint shop are 55 × 280 feet. The present car and blacksmith shop is 250 × 50 feet. Beside these are two large round-houses, one with stalls for fourteen locomotives, and the other with fourteen tracks for car repairs, and a drying kiln for lumber, 75 × 38 feet.

The transfer table, between the machine shop and blacksmith and car shops, is in three sections, which may be used jointly or separately, and two men can readily move a heavy locomotive to any point where it may be desirable to place it. Both broad and narrow gauge supply tracks run between the store room and machine shops. All the buildings are heated by steam in winter, and are so arranged with ventilators and sliding doors and windows, and are so lofty and airy, that the workmen are not annoyed by heat in summer. Seen from a distance the shops constitute a noticeable feature, being so arranged, with the tall chimneys and highest roofs, near the center, as to fall into a harmonious group, none the less picturesque and imposing in appearance because it is a temple of Vulcan.

DOWN THE LINE.

Leaving Denver the railway ascends the Platte valley eighteen miles to Acequia, passing Littleton, an important agricultural village, eleven miles from Denver. At Acequia it leaves the Platte, and follows the course of Plum Creek toward the divide. Castle Rock, the county-seat of Douglas county, thirty-three miles from Denver, is a flourishing village, surrounded by a good agricultural and grazing region. It takes its name from a picturesque, rock-crowned bluff near the town. Here are extensive quarries of a beautiful volcanic whitish-gray stone, much used for building purposes.

. The valleys of Plum Creek and its branches are quite wide, and are hollowed out of the modern deposits so as to form beautiful and fertile lands, while on each side a terrace extends down from the mountains, like a lawn. On either hand is a succession of high buttes and mesas, the lower portions being composed of sandstone, while the tops are of igneous rock, or lava. These constantly suggest artificial forms, towers, castles, fortifications, etc.; in some places rising nearly a thousand feet above the railway. Not unfrequently the cliffs are so regularly disposed that it is hard to believe them merely natural formations. Through and over these one occasionally catches a glimpse of Pike's Peak, or other heights of the snowy range. The entire scenery of this great ridge, or divide, and extending far out into the plains, is of a unique and interesting character. Near the summit there are remarkable evidences of its having been the coast line of an ancient sea, which must have covered all the plains.

On the summit, at the station called Divide, is a beautiful sheet of water, which has been named Palmer's Lake, in honor of the president of the company. It is remarkable as being one of the few lakes which, at high water, have outlets in two different directions. One, to the north, takes a part of its waters to the Platte, and thence to the Missouri, while the other, to the south, carries another portion to the Arkansas, and down to the Mississippi, so that in their flow they encompass a vast extent of territory.

Divide is 2,000 feet higher than Denver, and over 1,000 feet above Colo-

rado Springs. From Divide to the latter place the descent is rapid, and
the scenery all the way picturesque and attractive. The railway crosses a
corner of Monument Park, and for several miles there are scores of weird
and fantastic monument-like structures worn by the action of the elements
out of the soft sandstone of which the hills are composed. On the divide
and its outlying hills, in summer, there are sometimes violent rainstorms,
or "cloud-bursts," which convert every ravine and creek-bed into a raging
torrent, cutting deep gullies into the hillsides. Cherry Creek, taking its
rise in the Divide, and flowing through Denver, is usually merely a wide,
almost dry, creek-bed, but after one of these storms it is liable to be
changed in less than a moment from a streamlet that an infant might
safely cross to a torrent strong enough to overwhelm Pharaoh and his
hosts. The water comes down with a wall-like front, four or five feet
high, at almost the speed of a swift racer, and with a roaring sound that
may be heard for miles.
    The divide has a good covering of pines, often disposed by nature with
park-like symmetry, and forming a charming contrast with the bare but
beautifully colored cliffs; for at several places along the line may be seen,
looming up above the pines, immense cliffs of a bright red sandstone, while
others are gray, or white as chalk. This region has been the chief source
of the lumber supply. The timber tract is estimated to contain about
70,000 acres, some of the best of which has already been denuded of its
saw-timber. Monument, nineteen miles from Colorado Springs, is a considerable village, and has a good sized hotel, and numerous attractions as
a summer resort.
    Between Denver and Divide are several populous villages, which are
not shown on the maps, and at which the trains do not usually stop. The
production of bark is the chief occupation of their inhabitants, an industry
which may be considered hereditary with prairie dogs. They are curious
little animals, and sociable in their way.

COLORADO SPRINGS.

    In 1869 the lamented Horace Greeley, as a practical illustration of his
well-known advice to young men, decided to found an agricultural colony
in Colorado, and intrusted the choice of a location to Mr. Meeker and
General Cameron. The mountain base was examined from Pueblo to
Cheyenne. The Colorado Springs plateau, then a silent waste, was dis-
cussed and rejected, and the spot where Greeley now stands was finally
chosen. Greeley was a marked and rapid success.
    When the Denver and Rio Grande Railway Company began building
south from Denver its projectors determined to plant another colony, and
purchased for this purpose the discarded plateau at the foot of Pike's
Peak. They invited General Cameron to come and assist them; they
framed a colony organization, which prohibited the sale of intoxicating
liquors; and they inaugurated a very liberal system with reference to the

disposal of colony lots. Two thirds of all lots, uniformly distributed, were designated colony lots, and were sold to actual settlers at very low figures. The money so received, less a small percentage representing the actual cost of the land per acre, was devoted wholly to permanent improvements. Under this arrangement a fine irrigating canal, supplied both from the Fontaine-qui-Bouille and Monument creeks, was constructed; the streets were planted with long avenues of shade trees, which were watered by lateral ditches along each side of every street, and were well cared for year by year. Parks were laid out, fenced and planted, and an experimental garden was established. The railway company made its headquarters here, and gathered to this point a small and efficient staff, composed principally of young and enterprising Philadelphians. Nor was the British element altogether wanting, for the little group of pioneers have in vivid remembrance the tall, handsome form and Spanish features of Maurice Kingsley, the oldest son of the great author, and of his heroic and devoted sister, who fought out the coldest winter known in the annals of Colorado Springs in a thin board shanty far worse than a tent. The only other woman, be it recorded, at this early stage of the little colony, namely, that of Christmas, 1871, was Mrs. Giltner, who still presides over the little boot store which the early colony was so proud of.

The growth of the town at first was not as rapid as that of Greeley, but the little nucleus, on the principle that " birds of a feather flock together," gathered around it a number of cultivated and energetic people. By degrees the bright sunlight, the dry, healthy location of the town, its clean, well-kept streets and inviting residences, drew to it many who found that their physical condition required them to make a home for themselves in a mountain region. Thus the town grew and prospered. On July 31, 1871, the first frame house, if it deserves the name, was commenced. Now Colorado Springs contains 5,000 people, numerous churches and public buildings, including a beautiful stone college, a large school-house, and an Episcopal church, also of stone, several churches of wood, some of which are large edifices, the State Asylum for Deaf Mutes, and a well-constructed opera house, furnished with the latest stage appliances, similar to those of the Madison Square Theater, in New York. Many of the residences are well worthy of special notice, but we do not feel justified in giving undue publicity to the dwellings of private citizens. Colorado College was founded in 1874. The central block of the building is now completed, and the wings will soon be added. Both ladies and gentlemen are admitted. Only teachers of eminent ability are employed. The location is peculiarly adapted to the health of students, and to the pursuit of studies in natural science. The town is lighted with gas, and exceptionally well supplied with excellent water. This water is carried seven miles in pipes from Ruxton creek, which flows down one of the loveliest cañons above Manitou, where no impurities can ever reach it. The water arrives as clear as crystal, under high pressure; and, as no mechanical power is required, the water-rates are very low, and water is furnished gratuitously for fountains and garden purposes.

Colorado Springs is the capital of El Paso county, and is very likely to be chosen for the state capital. A magnificent site for state buildings has been set apart, covering ten acres, and is in process of adornment with trees and shrubs. The beautiful stone which is obtained from the Manitou quarries, and ranks highest among the many good building stones of the state in the Denver market, would form a fitting material for state buildings, and is used for all the choice structures in the town.

El Paso county is one of the richest in the state, and has always maintained a high credit. The first public work of importance was the construction of a free county road through the Ute Pass into the South Park, an undertaking both costly and difficult, but one which has contributed far more to the commercial prosperity of Colorado Springs than its originators ever anticipated; for during two years of the most active growth at Leadville, this excellent road induced most of the trade destined for California Gulch to seek Colorado Springs and the South Park route as the best highway to Leadville. The cattle interests of the county are important, and many of the chief cattle men have their residences at Colorado Springs. The same may be said of a number of gentlemen interested in the mines throughout the state, especially in Leadville and the San Juan country. Their families reside here.

There is a fine view of Pike's Peak from every part of Colorado Springs, but a still better one is obtained five miles farther off, to the northeast. Cheyenne Mountain, forming the southeastern extremity of the range, stands up in majestic grandeur in full view of the town, and is a "thing of beauty and a joy forever" to the inhabitants. The objects of interest in the vicinity are many, and the livery stables, which supply the means of visiting them, are numerous and excellent, for the best Kentucky stock, both for riding and driving, is owned by the livery men. To briefly enumerate the places best worth visiting we will begin south of the town, and progress to the east, north and west.

Bear Creek Cañon is reached by taking the road to Colorado City, and thence turning to the left. This is a beautiful drive of five miles, at the end of which the government trail to Pike's Peak carries pedestrians and horsemen to the summit. Bear Creek Cañon itself is a picturesque, wooded glen, with a dashing torrent, and abounds in wild flowers. Bears are still frequently seen here, and are much more alarmed at the stranger than the stranger has any reason to be at them.

The Cheyenne cañons are three and a half and four and a half miles distant. The road to these favorite resorts for picnic and pleasure parties starts in a southwesterly direction across the Fontaine, and is common to the two for two miles and a half, at which point it separates, the left road leading to South Cheyenne Cañon, the Cheyenne Mountain toll-road, and the seven lakes, and the road to the right leading to North Cheyenne

SEVEN FALLS, CHEYENNE CAÑON.

Cañon only, the more distant of the two.   Both these cañons are fine specimens of Rocky Mountain gorges. They are deeply cut into the sides of the beautiful mountain, and expose grand faces of magnificent red granite many hundred feet high. The Rocky Mountain pine, the Douglas spruce, the white spruce, and that most lovely tree of all, the Picea Grandis, grow luxuriantly in both cañons, while in the autumn season the Virginia creeper, two species of clematis (a mauve and a white), hop vines, and other climbers, lend a grace and charm to many a shady bower. North Cheyenne Cañon is the more open of the two, the stream is larger and more uproarious, and at many places the sides of the gorge can be easily climbed, and fine vistas thus obtained of the surrounding scenery. In South Cheyenne, on the contrary, the walls are very precipitous and imposing, and can only be scaled in one or two places by those accustomed to climbing. The stream, although smaller than its neighbor, forms, about two miles from its mouth, a fine cascade, falling about 500 feet in seven leaps.

The Cheyenne Mountain toll-road is well worth seeing. It ascends the mountains about one half mile south of the entrance to South Cheyenne Cañon, and winds for about ten miles, with easy grades, through very fine scenery, at times affording glimpses down into the cañon below.

The Seven Lakes are reached from the end of the above described road by means of a good horse-trail about ten miles long. The lakes are picturesque, as such sheets of water usually are among the mountains, and there is an inn for the accommodation of visitors.

" My Garden " is a very favorite resort, discovered by H. H., the authoress and poet. Take the Cheyenne road one and a half miles from Colorado Springs, then follow due south past Broad-Moor dairy farm half a mile, then through a gate across the " Big Hollow," and " My Garden " is reached, a lovely pine grove crowning a plateau, with an exquisite view of the range behind it.

Austin's Bluffs are five miles from Colorado Springs. Take the old Denver road, due north toward Templeton's Gap, for four miles, and then bear to the right into the Bluffs. There is no fear of missing the road, and when the Bluffs are reached not only does the plain present a limitless expanse, the influence of which few can behold unimpressed, but mountains hitherto unthought of suddenly appear. Apparently from the southern plains rise the twin heads of the Spanish Peaks, while the still loftier and more pointed crags, — the topmost summits of the Sangre de Cristo range, — uplift their snow-capped crests to the southwestern sky. The Spanish Peaks are a hundred miles distant; the tops of the Sangre de Cristo range which are visible from this point are at least thirty miles farther. They equal Pike's Peak in elevation, and really lie on the other side of the by no means insignificant chain of the Greenhorn Mountains, from behind which they rear their snow-clad summits.

Monument Park, eight miles northward, either by road or rail, and one

mile shorter by a bridle-path, is a very pleasant day's excursion. There
are here two comfortable houses for the accommodation of guests: Tea-
chout's, close to Egerton station, on the Denver and Rio Grande Railway,
and another higher up in the park. This place is chiefly remarkable for
the very fantastic forms into which time and the action of water have
worn the cream-colored sandstone rocks which the valleys have exposed,
forming grotesque groups of figures that very generally keep on their
broad-brimmed sombreros, doubtless for protection from the fierce rays of
the sun. In the group known as the "Dutch Wedding" most of the hats
have been doffed, we are told by a neighboring farmer, by the hands, not
of time, but of his boys. Those who take pleasure in inventing appropriate names for natural curiosities can here find a fertile field for their

GLEN EYRIE.

imaginations, and as the sandstone is very friable, and the outer coat
wears off every year, those who have a passion for carving their own
names everywhere can here do so with comparative impunity. We may
add, that although "stone-artists" are expressly forbidden, under heavy
fines and imprisonment by the laws of Colorado, from defacing the rocks
and trees of the country, no fierce limb of the law has yet been met footing

it through the secluded recesses of Monument Park. In Monument Park may be found splendid camping-grounds. Water, however, is scarce.

Douglas' Ranche, about a mile and a half nearer Colorado Springs, prettily situated among the foothills, is also a good camping place, and has abundance of water.

Blair Athol is located on a direct line between Douglas' Ranche and the entrance to Glen Eyrie, about one mile north of the latter, and three miles south of the former. Like Glen Eyrie, it is a large basin lying between the upturned reef of rocks which for hundreds of miles persistently skirts the eastern base of the Rocky Mountains, and generally known as the Hog-back, and the mountains themselves. The basin is entered by a rock portal, or narrow cleft in the Hog-back. Within are grouped in great confusion enormous pillars of exquisitely tinted pink sandstone, and huge slabs of similar material screen off chambers and secluded nooks, well fit for the haunts of ancient bandits or modern road agents. The place is extremely beautiful, and well worth seeing. No water is known to be found therein, although the entire basin, with its contents, has been carved out by its ever active agency.

One mile south of Blair Athol is the entrance to Glen Eyrie, which General Palmer, the president of this road, himself entered as his homestead and has made his home. It is watered by a rivulet, and is in many other respects superior to Blair Athol, although of exactly the same general character. Visitors were for years freely admitted, but the impossibility of preventing the privilege from being grossly abused in every possible way has obliged the owner to place restrictions on this permission.

The Garden of the Gods. So much has been said of this marvelous rock enclosure, and so many photographs have been taken of it, that all must be familiar with its general features. The photographs, however, fail to give any adequate idea of its gorgeous coloring, or of the noble view which its gateway frames. The best way to reach the Garden of the Gods from Colorado Springs is by what is known as the Mesa road, a beautiful drive of five miles. This road ascends the high table land, from which it derives its name, about one mile northwest of Colorado Springs, follows the perfectly level summit for three miles, and then descends the western side into the valley of Camp Creek by a broad carriage road cut in the hillside. On reaching the valley of Camp Creek, one mile down stream brings the visitor to the great gate of the Garden, which has been for some time in view from the top of the Mesa. After lingering for a few moments in front of the gateway, and enjoying the stately repose of Pike's Peak, as seen through and immediately in front of the gateway, he enters and continues his way toward Manitou, three miles beyond. The portals of this gateway are of massive red sandstone, 380 feet high. There is an outer parapet of white stone, and inner columns of various colors, which might well be the ruins of a vast heathen temple, or the shrine of the long buried gods. The impression produced by the Garden of the Gods varies

MANITOU AND PIKE'S PEAK.

greatly with the time of day and the climatic conditions under which it is
seen.   Immediately after rain its hues are deeper, and it becomes so
vividly red that an exact representation of it would be scouted at once as a
distorted vision of the painter.   In the soft light of evening a sagy green
of exquisite delicacy suffuses itself over the vegetation from which the
rocks in all directions rise; while the last rays of the departing sun cause
the enormous tablets of stone to flash out with surpassing grandeur.   As a
rule, to see the Garden to the best effect it should be approached from
Colorado Springs in the morning, and from Manitou at eventime.   If
possible, it should be visited at both times, and also by moonlight, when
the colors die away, and strange and almost unearthly forms take their
place.

BALANCED ROCK, GARDEN OF THE GODS.

COLORADO CITY,

the first capital of the territory, now a quiet little hamlet, between Colorado Springs and Manitou, was established when the fifty-niners first
came to Pike's Peak in their romantic quest for gold.   Failing to find it
at the foot of the Peak, they made their way through the Ute Pass, over
an almost impassable trail, thence across the South Park, and "struck it
rich" at last in Mosquito, Buckskin, and other ravines lying northward of
what is now Fairplay.   Descending from these high altitudes every autumn, they were accustomed to winter at Colorado City.   The glory of the

place has long since departed, and little of interest remains save reminiscences. The hewn-log house in which the first territorial legislature of Colorado assembled is still pointed out, but the hand of time lies heavily upon it.

Two and one-half miles west of Colorado City, and approached by a valley of gradually diminishing width and constantly increasing beauty, lies

PLUMB CRAGS, MANITOU.

MANITOU,

the most romantic and renowned watering-place of the Rocky Mountains, and the tourist center of Colorado. Here all information desired by sightseers and travelers about every part of the state is sedulously collected, and from this station special tourist tickets will be issued during the season to all points of interest on the Denver and Rio Grande Railway system. In 1880 the railway company constructed a branch to Manitou.

In locating the line great care was taken not to mar the beauty of the valley, nor interfere with driving on the main road. The company proposes to beautify the land belonging to it on each side of the track between Manitou and Colorado Springs, and make it a model pleasure road. Five passenger trains are run each way daily, supplied with drawing-room cars free of extra charge.

For a brief description of Manitou and its springs we cannot do better than quote from a pamphlet by Dr. S. Edwin Solly:

" Manitou is situated in a beautiful valley among the foot-hills of the Rocky Mountains, at an elevation of 6,297 feet. It is the gate, as it were, of the Ute Pass, which cuts westward through the spur of the main chain, of which Pike's Peak is the highest point, lying to the northern side and almost beneath the shadow of this grand mountain. It is seventy-five miles south of Denver, the capital of Colorado, and five miles west of the prosperous town of Colorado Springs, which stands four hundred feet below it, on the opening plateau of the great plains, from whence the Denver and Rio Grande Railway connects it with Denver in the north and New Mexico in the south. This valley stands at an altitude of 6,370 feet above sea level, and 8,000 feet below the summit of Pike's Peak.

" Most of the mineral springs are to be found among the picturesque windings of the Fountain Creek, a clear, fast-running stream, with a rocky bed, which comes down from the mountain through the Ute Pass. The mineral springs that are at present used are six in number. They vary in temperature from 43° to 56° F., and are strongly charged with carbonic acid. Coming up the valley the first is the Shoshone, bubbling up under a wooden canopy, in the middle of the main road of the village, and often called the Sulphur Spring from the yellow deposit left around it. A few yards further on, and in a ledge of rock overhanging the right bank of the Fountain, is the Navajo, abounding in carbonates of soda, lime and magnesia, and still more strongly charged with carbonic acid, having a refreshing taste similar to seltzer water. From this rocky basin pipes conduct the water to the bath-house, which is situated on the stream a little further down. Crossing by a pretty rustic bridge we come to the Manitou, close to an ornamental summer-house; its taste and properties closely resemble the Navajo. Recrossing the stream and walking about a quarter of a mile up the Ute Pass road, following the right bank of the Fountain, we find, close to its brink, the Ute Soda. This resembles the Manitou and Navajo, but is chemically less powerful, though much enjoyed for a refreshing draught. Retracing one's steps to within two hundred yards of the Manitou Spring, we cross a bridge leading over a stream which joins the Fountain at almost a right angle from the southwest; following up the right bank of this mountain brook, which is called Ruxton's Creek, we enter the most beautiful of the tributary valleys of Manitou; traversing the winding road among rocks and trees for nearly half a mile, we reach a summer-house close to the right bank of the creek, in which we find the

Iron Ute, the water being highly effervescent, of the temperature of 44.°3′ F., and very agreeable in spite of its marked chalybeate taste. Continuing up the left bank of the stream for a few hundred yards, we reach the last of the springs that have been analyzed — the Little Chief; this is less agreeable in taste, being less effervescent and more strongly impregnated with sulphate of soda than any of the other springs, and containing nearly as much iron as the Iron Ute.

UTE IRON SPRINGS — PIKE'S PEAK TRAIL.

"These springs have from time immemorial enjoyed a reputation as healing waters among the Indians, who, when driven from the glen by the inroads of civilization, left behind them wigwams to which they used to bring their sick; believing, as they did, that the Good Spirit breathed into the waters the breath of life, they bathed and drank of them, thinking thereby to find a cure for every ill; yet it has been found that they thought most highly of their virtue when their bones and joints were racked with pain, their skins covered with unsightly blotches, or their warriors weakened by wounds or mountain sickness. During the seasons that the use of these waters has been under observation, it has been noticed that rheumatism, certain skin diseases and cases of debility have been much benefited, so far confirming the experience of the past. The Manitou and

Navajo have also been highly praised for their relief of old kidney and liver troubles, and the Iron Ute for chronic alcoholism and uterine derangements. Many of the phthisical patients who come to this dry, bracing air in increasing numbers are also said to have drank of the waters with evident advantage.

"Professor Loew (chemist to the Wheeler expedition), speaking of the Manitou Springs as a group, says, very justly, they resemble those of Ems, and excel those of Spa — two of the most celebrated groups in Europe.

"On looking at the analyses of the Manitou group it will be seen that they all contain carbonic acid and carbonate of soda, yet they vary in some of their other constituents. We will, therefore, divide them into three groups of carbonated soda waters. 1. The carbonated soda waters proper, comprising the Navajo, Manitou and Ute Soda, in which the soda and carbonic acid have the chief action. 2. The purging carbonated soda waters, comprising the Little Chief and Shoshone, where the action of the soda and carbonic acid is markedly modified by the sulphates of soda and potash. 3. The ferruginous carbonated soda waters, where the action of the carbonic acid and soda is modified by the carbonate of iron, comprising the Iron Ute and the Little Chief, which latter belongs to this group as well as to the preceding one."

EXCURSIONS.

A very pleasant feature of Manitou is that, within a short walk of any of the hotels, one enters the mountains by deep cañons of great interest and beauty. The most favorite mountain rides are:

To the summit of Pike's Peak, easily accomplished, with return, in ten hours of daylight. Parties often start early in the afternoon, and ride to the Lake House, about at timber line, where they stop for the night, and reach the top of the Peak by sunrise, getting back to Manitou about noon. The Lake House furnishes comfortable private bedrooms, and good plain fare. Pike's Peak is 14,147 feet in altitude. The distance from Manitou to the summit is thirteen miles.

To Crystal Park, a delightful morning or afternoon horseback excursion. This should be the first trip taken, because in going there the visitor gets a general view of the country around, which he can afterward explore for a fortnight without being wearied.

To the Seven Lakes, by the beautiful Cheyenne Mountain road. This excursion is a very enjoyable one, and there is a good inn at the lakes, where the visitor can stop for the night. This trip can be made in a carriage as soon as the present road is completed a few miles further.

Lying back, on the south side of Manitou valley, are high ridges, which are easily reached on horseback by ascending the cañon in which the stone quarry is situated. These ridges can be followed for miles, and the views therefrom of mountain and defile are never to be forgotten.

The cañons best worth visiting are, the Manitou (or Williams'), immediately at the rear of the Cliff House. To see the best part of it the visitor should have perseverance enough to ascend it for three miles, two miles of which can be accomplished in a carriage. Cheyenne Cañons are situated in Cheyenne Mountain, seven miles from Manitou by road, or three and one-half miles from Colorado Springs. They are two in number: Cheyenne and North Cheyenne, the latter one mile farther to the left. Both are very beautiful. North Cheyenne is probably the most picturesque, but the other has a grand waterfall, in which the cascade makes seven leaps in a height of about 500 feet.

Beside the above named localities Ute Pass and Rainbow Falls should be visited, as well as the Garden of the Gods.

RAINBOW FALLS IN WINTER.

A very pleasant change, particularly in warm weather, is a trip to Manitou Park. The Rocky Mountains contain, in various places, beautiful parks, surrounded by pine forests, flanked by mountains, which parks are really the dry beds of ancient lakes. A good example of these is the park in question. A drive of twenty-one miles over an exceptionally good road, up through the Ute Pass and across the divide, brings one to the

Park Hotel, beautifully situated in the center of a park having an elevation of 7,800 feet. This little hotel has good accommodations for about thirty visitors, and has a livery stable and dairy farm attached. The air here is particularly light and bracing, and the odors of the pine forests are considered very beneficial to those who, unfortunately, have weak lungs. A trout stream runs through the park, upon which there is a regular fish-breeding establishment, where the proprietor has for years been cultivating the *Fontinalis*, or eastern mountain trout. The especial advantage claimed for this trout over the Rocky Mountain variety is that, spawning in the winter, it is in season in summer, whereas the native Colorado trout, as it spawns late in the spring, is not in season until October. The *Fontinalis* is also a more lively and crafty fish, and therefore, although it requires a better sportsman to catch it, it is more likely to hold its own, while the Colorado trout is fast disappearing from the mountain streams in which, a few years ago, it was very abundant. Again, spawning late in the spring, the eggs of the native trout are destroyed in great numbers by the freshets of early summer, caused by rapidly melting mountain snows. The eggs of the *Fontinalis*, on the contrary, are protected in midwinter by the ice-covering of the streams, and are hatched and out of danger before the snow begins to melt in the mountains. A lake of fourteen acres is now heavily stocked with the *Fontinalis*, and a good fly fisher can catch twenty pounds of them almost any evening about sundown. In the fall Manitou Park is a good headquarters for deer-stalking, and those who hunt in the neighborhood find the deer about as plentiful as formerly. Mountain grouse, although not numerous, are generally to be found on those highest ridges which are covered with pine or spruce. They are such handsome birds that a good walker will find it worth while to hunt them.

HOTELS.

Perhaps no factor contributes more prominently to the popularity of a health or pleasure resort than its hotels, and in this particular Manitou presents superior attractions.

The Beebee House is beautifully located, and is the largest and finest hotel in the vicinity of the Rocky Mountains. It has a frontage of 280 feet, and contains 150 guests' chambers, a ball-room 30 × 50 feet in size, a dining-room of quaint design, 35 × 60 feet, music-room, 20 × 34 feet, two spacious parlors, a billiard-room, 70 feet long, bowling-alleys, etc. It is fitted with new and costly furniture, and velvet, Turkish and Brussels carpets. Hot and cold water is supplied in pipes to every part of the house. Its wide and pleasant verandas afford over 600 feet of space, sheltered from the sun, and in full view of the mountains.

The Manitou House is situated near the Beebee House, Grace Greenwood's cottage occupying the grounds between. It contains 100 rooms for guests, and is well supplied with modern luxuries and conveniences. Its grounds are especially admired, being shaded with trees and adorned with

WILLIAMS' CAÑON.

grass-plat and fountain. The Fontaine-qui-Bouille dashes through them. The piazza is a marked feature, being 180 feet long, and very wide. A beautiful view of Pike's Peak is obtained from it, and here the visitors watch the sun set behind the mountains in the summer evenings, and enjoy the cooling zephyrs, fragrant with wild flowers.

The Cliff House is a good hotel, with less pretensions, and situated nearest the soda springs. And there are also several excellent boarding-houses in different parts of the village.

Manitou is well supplied with livery-stables, there being four well stocked establishments; and hardly less prominent is the Pike's Peak burro train.

FROM COLORADO SPRINGS TO SOUTH PUEBLO,

a distance of forty-five miles, the railway traverses the fertile, alluvial valley of the Fontaine-qui-Bouille. The plains extend to the east, and the mountains, of which Cheyenne is the most prominent, form the western façade, at first extending north and south, but farther south receding to form the deep cove at the upper end of which lies Cañon City. For a short distance the snowy pinnacles of the Sangre de Cristo range can be seen above the lower summits of the Greenhorn Mountains. This view is obtained from a point about about fifteen miles below Colorado Springs, and the traveler must be on the lookout or he will probably fail to see them.

SOUTH PUEBLO AND PUEBLO,

practically one city, though supporting two municipal organizations, being only separated by the Arkansas river, are important, prosperous and grow-ing towns, which, for the purposes of this work, may properly be treated together. Their location, from a commercial point of view, is one of the most advantageous in the state. Here is the junction of the great eastern trunk line, the Atchison, Topeka and Santa Fé Railroad, with three divi-sions of the Denver and Rio Grande Railway, whose score of branches ramify through the vast mining districts of Colorado. There is much fer-tile land near South Pueblo, with abundance of water, and excellent facilities for irrigation. It is also surrounded with rich pasture lands, upon which immense herds of cattle and sheep roam at large, watched by mounted cow-boys and patient herders. On the mesas or table-lands near South Pueblo is a beautiful tract, of great extent and nearly level, which furnishes an excellent location for residences. Pueblo is the county-seat of Pueblo county, and the site of the State Asylum for the Insane. It has two daily and several weekly newspapers.

As a manufacturing city South Pueblo promises to become noted. Here is located the extensive establishment known as the Pueblo Smelting and Refining Works, already among the first in the state in its production of bullion. These works are being rapidly enlarged, and employ a great number of men.

The Colorado Coal and Iron Company has selected South Pueblo as the site of an establishment for the manufacture of Bessemer steel from the crude iron, and is erecting works on a large scale, with capacity for producing 30,000 tons of steel rails per annum, and capable of such further extension as may be necessary. One large hot-blast iron furnace, 65 feet high, 15 boshes, with three Siemens-Cowper-Cochrane heating stoves, 58 feet high by 15 feet in diameter, and a brick hoist-tower, boiler, engine and casting-houses complete, have been erected, with the intention of having the furnace in blast early in the summer of 1881. A stone machine-shop, 48 × 104 feet, and a stone foundry, 50 × 50 feet, are finished and in operation. Around these works will naturally spring up other manufactories of iron and steel, such as car-wheels, engines, hoisters, pumps, mining machinery, stoves, iron pipe, horse-shoes, nails, etc. The company owns the mines necessary for a supply of coal and iron, both being situated within easy reach of the furnaces. On Grape Creek, between Cañon City and Silver Cliff, it has 1,057 acres, known as Iron Mountain, a large deposit of magnetic iron ore, and near South Arkansas, the Calumet, Hecla and Smithville iron mines. Besides these are several valuable leases, and a number of mines yet undeveloped on different branches of the Denver and Rio Grande Railway. Its coal fields at El Moro, Cuchara and Cañon City embrace 13,571 acres.

OLD BALAAM.

Where great Pike's Peak his summit rears
  'Mid foot-hills robed in richest brown,
And o'er the Great Plains proudly peers—
  A monarch he with snowy crown,—
There, high above the ocean's tides,
A famed, historic mule resides,

Upon the Peak's supremest height,
　　Brave men a tireless vigil keep;
'Tis they who, with unerring sight,
　　Spy storms afar that onward sweep,
And herald to the world below
When sun shall shine or tempest blow.

From plain to mountain's crest there leads,
　　Round cliff and chasm's brink, a trail;
Sure feet, indeed, the creature needs
　　Who safe the dizzy heights would scale,
Where one false step the wretch might throw
O'er precipice to death below.

Of all the beasts that climb this trail,
　　'Tis Balaam (so our mule is named)
Whose history forms the strangest tale,
　　Whose exploits are so justly famed —
" Old Prob's " most trusty delegate,
Far Western things to regulate.

For full eight years has Balaam toiled
　　This signal service to perform,
His coat with dust of summer soiled,
　　His marrow chilled by wintry storm;
And now old age comes on apace,
But finds of waning powers no trace.

This ancient, grizzled mule I sought,
    If haply he'd be interviewed;
Since sure in Holy Writ 'tis taught,
    How, where the barring angel stood,
A prophet, who was sure no saint,
Had listened to an ass's plaint.

Perhaps long residence on heights,
    Where all know that the air is thin,
May have induced the airy flights
    Of romance this mule reveled in,
Or mighty sweep of range and plain
Have gauged the workings of his brain.

But sure it is no poet's ear
    E'er listened to a stranger tale;
The rocks re-echoed far and near,
    The poet's face grew ashy pale,
As Balaam brayed sonorously
His most astounding history.

He told of high-born ancestry,
    Of noble sire and gentle dam,
Brothers and sisters, gay and free,
    And his young life so bright and calm;
He traced a long, unbroken line
Of proud relations asinine,

Ambitions soon this scion seized
    Which amply proved his pedigree;
He would go West, were parents pleased,
    The Great Plains and the mountains see;
Nor should he e'er in quiet rest
Till he had climbed the Rocky's crest.

That he, this scheme which genius shows,
    Found ways and means to carry out,
No one who mulish methods knows
    Could ever have a lingering doubt.
It may suffice us now to say
That, like all mules, he had his way.

So now, his true vocation found,
    He started on a proud career;
From plain to summit, safe and sound,
    He carried hundreds every year—
Ladies who shrieked at steep ascent,
And many a scared but silent gent.

All this and more Old Balaam tells,
    And feels his youth renewed thereby;
But now his bray in anger swells
    And viciously his heels do fly,
While laboring to me to rehearse
    His shameful wrongs in halting verse,

" I was a faithful mule," he said,
    "And meant to do the honest thing;
How was I shocked, one night in bed,
    To hear a sharp, resounding ring
That said, by click of telegraph,
My feed must be reduced one half!

" The civil service, so it said,
    At last had got to be reformed,
A start must somewhere soon be made,
    This citadel corrupt be stormed;
But, since big guns might fire back,
They'd try at first a Pike's Peak jack.

"All this was too much to be borne;
    My plans with lightning speed were made,
And I was free before the morn,
    Escaped by strategy deep laid,
And guided to the plains below
By the volcano's lurid glow.

" When I was down scarce half the way,
    Three mountain lions gave me chase,
I met them: one yet lives, they say,
    The rest in fragments sail through space!
All who have seek my backward reach
Will know that solemn truth I teach,

" This victory gained, I came to where
　　A stream of lava crossed the trail;
The fiery current singed my hair,
　　I labored, but without avail,
To cross the seething, boiling tide
That must have been full ten yards wide.

"At last I spied a pine-crowned hill,
　　O'ertopping quite the highest flame;
Upon its crest I waited till
　　A ' Colorado zephyr ' came,
Then with my ample ears set sail,
And over sped before the gale!

" So now I'm on my way to see
　　The head men of the Narrow Gauge;
If they'll but listen to my plea
　　And these my burning wrongs assuage,
Between us yet, I have no fears,
We'll take the whole world by the ears.

" I'll ask them to extend their rail
　　Clear to the summit of the Peak,
Run opposition to the trail,
　　And all that Signal Service clique;
' Old Prob' shall yet bewail the day
When he put Balaam on half-pay.

"The Rio Grande runs, I hear,
   O'er cloud-wrapped summits, 'mid the snow,
Clambers where mountain sheep might fear,
   Or winds through cañons far below.
Success shall yet my efforts crown;
Farewell, I'm off for Denver town!"

With heels and tail aloft in air,
   Old Balaam scampers o'er the plain,
While lifts the poet's conscious hair
   And wildly throbs his swelling brain,
At thoughts of what e'en mules may dare
In this great country of light air!

PUEBLO TO LEADVILLE.

FROM South Pueblo the Denver and Rio Grande Railway follows the
course of the Arkansas river forty-one miles to Cañon City. The trend of the
valley is a little north of west, and the stream cuts through mesas of hard
clay and sandstone, which form perpendicular banks, or palisades, usually
at some distance from the river. This valley is much the warmest portion
of the state, the snowfall in winter being very slight, and the wind seldom
severe. In summer the heat is sometimes oppressive, owing to the char-

SCENE IN PUEBLO.

acter of the soil and the surrounding elevations, which are a barrier to the
winds. It is the only valley in Colorado where Indian corn reaches its
full size and is a standard crop. The line of the railway is in places very
picturesque. It crosses the Arkansas several times, opening up beautiful
vistas, dives in and out of thick groves of fine old cottonwoods, skirts the
immediate edge of the rapidly running river, and anon gracefully curves
round a massive pile of rocks and loses itself in the shrubbery.

CAÑON CITY.

At the head of a great cove in the front range of the Rocky Mountains,
between the Greenhorn Mountains and the ranges south of the South Park,
and just below where the Arkansas river plunges through a chasm half a
mile deep in the solid granite to enter upon its almost interminable journey across the plains, lies Cañon City, a substantial town of over 2,000

inhabitants, and the county-seat of Fremont county. Here the Westcliffe division branches off to the south and west to supply the Wet Mountain Valley, Silver Cliff and Rosita.

Some ten miles to the southeast, reached by a branch track, are the Cañon City coal mines, which produce a superior quality of coal that commands the highest price of any in the state. The production of these mines during the winter averages about six hundred tons per day. The oil springs, near Cañon City, have been known for the past seventeen years, and during that time have yielded several hundred barrels of oil per annum, surface flow. Numerous borings were made near them without result till, in February, 1881, oil was struck, at a depth of 1,450 feet, in a well near the coal mines. The capacity of the well will be learned as soon as the proper machinery is in operation.

The mineral springs at Cañon City, both warm and cold, are regarded as among the most valuable in the state. The water of the cold springs is almost icy in temperature, and strongly impregnated with soda. The hot springs are recommended for cutaneous and blood diseases. They are supplied with good bathing facilities. The state penitentiary is located at Cañon City. The buildings and walls are of stone from extensive quarries near the prison, and convict labor is employed in dressing stone for building purposes.

THE WESTCLIFFE DIVISION.

One mile west from Cañon City, near the entrance to the Grand Cañon of the Arkansas, the Westcliffe Division leaves the Leadville Division, and follows the course of Grape Creek to Westcliffe, thirty-two miles to the southwest, and two miles from Silver Cliff. Soon after diverging this division enters

GRAPE CREEK CAÑON.

Among the many remarkable cañons for which the State of Colorado is famous, there is probably none which presents more attractions to the lover of nature, or which combines the sublime with the beautiful more perfectly, than that of Grape Creek. This beautiful stream takes its rise among the lofty and almost inaccessible peaks of the Sangre de Cristo range, and flowing nearly northward waters in its course the beautiful and fertile Wet Mountain Valley; then passing near the famous Silver Cliff mining camp it continues its tortuous course in an easterly direction until it enters the Arkansas river about a mile above Cañon City, just where the river leaves the Grand Cañon, after its terrific conflict with the granite cliffs, and tossing its foam-crests high in air, makes its last triumphant exit from the mountains. The creek receives its name from the profusion of wild grape vines, which, sheltered by the lofty rock walls, grow luxuriantly upon their lower slopes and relieve the ruggedness of their abrupt steeps, as if nature found she had done her work too roughly, and then veiled it with flowers and clinging vines. The walls of this cañon present a splendid study for the geologist, as piled up in many places over a thousand feet in nearly vertical height, they exhibit the various formations of primary rock in a striking and peculiar manner. The entrance to the cañon for over a mile follows the windings of the clear flowing creek, with gently sloping hills on either side covered with low spruce and piñon, and with grass plats and brilliant flowers in season far up their slopes, and the Spanish lance and bush cactus present their bristling points wherever a little soil affords them sustenance.

At a sharp bend about a mile up the creek a trail leading to the left for a few hundred yards reveals on the side of the cliff a singular formation of varicolored rocks in perfect strata, dipping at an angle of about forty-five degrees from the top of the mountain to the level of the pass before us, like a mighty ribbon of red, brown and white stripes, while the formation crosses the trail like a wall built by Titan hands. Returning and following up the creek we make another sharp turn, and come in view of lofty cliffs of red and gray granite, in which great seams of black trap-rock cross in diagonal lines, and at their base the streamlet has hollowed out deep pools, clear as crystal, in whose shadows the timid trout love to hide. Then you see these great cliffs, rent with awful chasms dark and fathomless, and as you watch you almost expect to see the forms of the genii of the mountains shape themselves out of the nebulous darkness. A dim yet mighty consciousness of power vast and measureless, before which human thought recoils, grows upon you as you stand in the presence of the ages, before which the pride of human power is dwarfed. In several places in the cañon, where the walls seem high and solid, streams from above have, during long ages, cut deep vertical passages like open gates, narrow and smooth, with irregular steps up which one may climb, and he finds behind them little parks filled with broken rock, between which a wilderness of green has grown, and flowers bloom which are rarely seen by human eyes. Only the sun and the nightly stars and birds enjoy their beauty.

The constantly winding valley is sometimes narrowed so as to give scarcely a passage. At other points it widens into grass-covered and well-shaded parks. It is impossible to picture in detail, in a work like this, nor indeed can pencil describe, the kaleidoscopic changes which are revealed at every turn of this beautiful valley. There is one place, however, a little distance from the road, which every tourist should visit. About seven miles from the mouth of the creek, a small branch cañon comes in from the right. It was once a deep cleft, with perpendicular sides, created in some convulsion of nature, but it has been gradually filled up with débris and broken rock until a sloping and not difficult path is made, by the sides of which a luxuriant vegetation has taken root, and the wild rose and clematis blooms with the humble blue-bell among the mossy boulders. Climbing this path for a few hundred feet a side cleft is seen at the right, which seems to terminate in a solid wall. Following it to the breast, however, you find at the left a passage made by a water channel, with steps

which ladies can easily pass with a little help, and we enter a narrow passage between high rocky walls. Turning again to the right, we follow this
perhaps two hundred feet, and looking to the left we find before and above
us the lofty arched dome of the " Temple." About twenty-five feet above
where we are standing is a platform, perhaps fifty feet in width and six or
eight feet in depth, over which projects far above the arching roof.
Though the auditorium in front is rather narrow for a great audience, the
platform is grand, and may be reached without great difficulty. Music
sounds finely as it rolls down from the overhanging sounding-board of
stone. From the platform deep cavernous recesses are seen at the sides,
which time has wrought, but which are invisible from below. Moreover,
the action of water slowly percolating through the back walls, carrying
lime and spar in solution, has coated them with crystals, which gleam in
sparkling beauty when the sunlight touches them early in the day. Farther up the cañon the rocks do not rise to so great heights, and the vista
opens out into pleasant winding valleys well covered with grass, but there
are several very interesting points where the action of internal convulsions
upon the granite and sienite in elder ages, when they came hot from the
crucible of nature, have rolled and twisted and kneaded the great rock
masses into most curious and notable shapes.

To examine this cañon thoroughly a carriage or saddle-horses should
be taken from Cañon City, but, as the train ascent of the grades must be
made slowly, a very satisfactory view can be gained from the cars in passing. It makes a most charming and picturesque ride, the only regret concerning which is that amid such beauty and grandeur the time flies too
swiftly by, and only the pictures of memory are left.

After passing out of Grape Creek Cañon the railway emerges into the

WET MOUNTAIN VALLEY,

an ancient lake basin lying between the Greenhorn Mountains and Sangre
de Cristo range. The average elevation of this valley is 7,800 feet. It is
about twenty-five miles long, and the level bottom land in the widest part
is fully five miles across. It is probably the finest body of hay land that
has been settled in Colorado, and is covered with well fenced ranches.
The first settlement was made in 1870, since which time all the arable land
has been taken up. It is drained by Grape creek, which passes through
the deep cañon just described, twenty miles in length, before reaching the
Arkansas. Its situation separated it so completely from the more thickly
peopled centers that the farming population, although attracted at first by
the richness of the soil, found it hard to make their produce profitable.
Such was the condition of affairs when silver mines were discovered on
the west slope of the Greenhorn Mountains, and the beautiful little mining
town of Rosita was formed. This was in 1873. The next important discovery was made in 1877, when the Bassick gold mine was found, about
two miles north of Rosita. This mine appears to be the crater of an

extinct mud volcano, the ore having been deposited on the outside of boulders as the volcano gradually ceased to be active. All through that country there are evidences of deposits from hot mineral springs and other
recent volcanic phenomena. The year following three discouraged miners
thought they would have a piece of rock from a cliff which looked like
common sand-rock, partially burnt, assayed, and they found to their surprise that it contained silver. The names of these men were Powell,
Haffard, and Edwards. On further examination a large portion of the cliff
was found to be impregnated with chloride of silver. The cliff, however,
is considered by geologists to consist of porphyry, although it closely
resembles sandstone. Around the cliff a mining town sprang up with
extraordinary rapidity, to which was given the appropriate name of

SILVER CLIFF.

The city of Silver Cliff is situated on the plateau near the foot of Round
Mountain, at the eastern side of the valley, two miles east of Westcliffe, the
terminus of the Denver and Rio Grande Railway. It sprang up almost
instantaneously, its growth being stimulated by the discovery of new
mines, and has already come to be the third town in population within the
state. It is beautifully located and regularly laid out, and, although most
of the buildings are of wood, it presents a more homelike appearance than
most new towns. The young city already boasts of Holly water-works, in
successful operation, which were constructed at a cost of $75,000. The
water is taken from springs in the vicinity, and is excellent in quality. A
gas company has been organized, and the stock all subscribed, ready to
begin operations in a short time. Two daily and several weekly newspapers furnish the news to an intelligent and wide-awake community.
Schools and churches have kept pace with its rapid material growth, and
its people claim that it surpasses other rapidly built mining towns in the
number of its homes and the character of its society. The altitude of Silver Cliff is 7,816 feet.

There are in and around Silver Cliff five stamp-mills (two of forty
stamps each and one of eighty stamps), and concentrating works capable
of concentrating 150 tons of ore per day. The mine to which these works
are attached is a large deposit of argentiferous galena, while the chloride
ores are milling ores, containing an average of $20 to the ton.

WESTCLIFFE,

the railway terminus, is beautifully situated on the upland overlooking the
valley, and facing the Sangre de Cristo range, being separated from it by
an unbroken stretch of four miles of farming land. The green fields and
farm buildings dotted all over the fertile valley, the meandering streams
and the snow-capped peaks beyond, form a combination of repose and
grandeur seldom met with. Behind Westcliffe, covering a semicircle of
hills about six miles across, are the mines of the district, which already

support a population of over 6,000 people. The town site is mostly covered by a large irrigating canal, taken from Grape creek, six miles above the town. The water from this canal will be carried by means of lateral ditches down both sides of every street, and will water the trees and gardens. The Holly water-works are situated in the southwest corner of town, and the main supply-pipe runs through the center. The railway station is located at the west end, about one-fourth of a mile from Grape creek. The railway company contemplates the erection of several buildings here corresponding with the importance of the town. Among other projected improvements of interest to the traveler is the erection of a magnificent hotel, in connection with the railway depot, having a frontage of 350 feet, facing the range and overlooking the valley.

The depot is at a point in the valley from which the produce of the mines on both sides, and the mills located along Grape creek and elsewhere, will be most easily supplied. The road from Rosita passes, by a gradual descent for seven miles, down to this point. No more favorable location could be selected for the convenience of the entire district.

ROSITA.

The beautiful and prosperous mining town of Rosita lies six miles southeast of Silver Cliff, and is the center of what has been known as the Hardscrabble Mining District. It numbers nearly 2,000 inhabitants. Rosita is surrounded by valuable mining properties, and cannot fail to increase in wealth and population. The altitude is 500 feet greater than that of Silver Cliff. Rosita was a center of great mining activity before Silver Cliff was founded, and it yet retains its distinction of being the county-seat of Custer county, which was organized in 1877

SCENERY AND SURROUNDINGS.

We must not leave the Wet Mountain valley without a passing notice of its scenery. Prof. Hayden, whose word is certainly second to none, considers the view of the Sangre de Cristo range from the opposite side of Wet Mountain Valley, in the month of June, while sufficient snow still remains on the highest peaks to make them effective, the grandest view of the kind in Colorado. The peaks of this portion of the range are very lofty; four of them exceed in elevation, Pike's Peak; and the average height of the crest is about 13,000 feet. A visitor wishing to corroborate Prof. Hayden's opinion as to the beauty of the mountain views, has only to drive along the road from Silver Cliff direct to Rosita, or to watch the sunset from the heights of Westcliffe.

The farms near Westcliffe are noted throughout the state. The Clifton hay farm embraces about 2,000 acres, 1,600 of which are enclosed by good fences. It is under a thorough system of irrigation, and produces about 1,000 tons of hay and 5,000 bushels of oats each season.

Returning to Canon City, the Leadville division of the Denver and Rio Grande Railway bears the traveler westward and immediately into the

GRAND CAÑON OF THE ARKANSAS, AND ROYAL GORGE.

Of all the deep cañons penetrated by railways on either continent, the Grand Cañon of the Arkansas is the most wonderful and the most celebrated. For years before the railway was built, it was customary for people to drive over the mountains from Cañon City, and peer down into the Royal Gorge. One writer, in describing his first view from above, says: "Cowards at heart, pale of face, and with painful breath, we slowly crawl on hands and knees to the ledge, and as the fated murderer feels the knotted noose fall down over his head, so we feel as our eyes extend beyond the rocks to catch one awful glimpse of the eternity of space. Few dare to look more than once, and one glance suffices for a comprehension of the meaning of the word depth never before dreamed of and never afterward forgotten. The gorge is 3,000 feet sheer depth, and the most pricipitous and sublime in its proportions of any chasm on the continent. The opposite wall towers hundreds of feet above us, and if possible to imagine anything more terrifying than the position on this side, that upon the other would be were its brink safe to approach." We cannot refrain from quoting from another description, by Grace Greenwood, who writes: "I was lost in silent joy when I came to look down in that Grand Cañon, the greatest sight I have yet seen in Colorado. It is grander than the Yosemite, because of its color, which is everywhere dark with rich porphyry tints. So awful was the chasm, so stupendous were the mountain steeps around it, so gloomy were the woods, so strange, and lonely, and savage and out of the world seemed the whole vast scene, that it recalled to me the passage in the ' Inferno ':

> 'There is a place within the depths of hell
>   Called Malebolge, all rock. dark stained,
> With hue ferruginous, e'en as the steep
>   That round it circling winds. Right in the midst
> Of that abominable region yawns
>   A spacious gulf profound.'

"This great sight ought to draw thousands of tourists to Cañon. I am amazed that there is no more said of it and written about it. To me it is infinitely more impressive than Niagara."

The entrance to the Grand Cañon is one mile above Cañon City. A narrow mountain spur extends down nearly to the river, abruptly terminating in a granite promontory, the face of which, toward the valley, is a sheer precipice some 200 feet in height, constituting an imposing "sentinel rock." Near this is the mouth of Grape Creek, and directly opposite the track of the Westclifle Division crosses the Arkansas upon a long truss bridge, while the main line rounds the promontory and enters upon the constantly narrowing and deepening labyrinths of the Grand Cañon. As

ROYAL GORGE.

it gets farther into the cañon, the walls on either side grow higher and appear more stern and forbidding. On the benches, close by the track, are seen hundreds of specimens of the bush cactus, holding a place among plants similar to that of the porcupine among animals. A little back, the enclosing granite walls rise, height above height, in a succession of craggy ledges, split and shattered, seamed with fissures and broken with gorges. In these fissures and on the tops of the ledges, often with no apparent soil to sustain them, are gnarled and rugged cedars. Frequently through some narrow cleft in the top of a ledge one catches glimpses of a much higher ledge beyond, with cedars clinging to its loftiest crags. Thus far its appearance is similar to that of other cañons, elsewhere in the state, that are far-famed for their scenery; but as the railway penetrates deeper into the mountains, all other cañons are forgotten in the overwhelming grandeur of the granite barriers that narrow toward the Royal Gorge. The cañon is here a mere fissure, and the river, crowded between the walls, and broken into foam by the rocks that have fallen into its bed, occupies one side, while the railway track, ten or twelve feet above it, lies close against the opposite wall, save where for a few rods the walls recede a little, enabling the eye to follow their surface to the topmost crags, 3,000 feet above. The rocks are many-hued: bright red, green, grayish white, and brown; here stained with dropping water, and there overgrown with moss. Imprisoned in this narrow space, so crooked that the walls seem to close behind and before, the traveler who first beholds the scene from the platform of a swift passing car is bewildered with the kaleidoscopic changes. Here a smooth surface of granite, perpendicular for over a thousand feet; there a point so splintered and wrecked that it seems about to fall; reaching so far upward that the imagination stands appalled and struggles in vain to realize the awful height. Now the train is under the face of a cliff that has been cut into to make a roadbed, chipped off for several hundred feet above by workmen who drilled into the granite while suspended in the air by ropes let down from the top, and now it sweeps past the mouth of a gorge that runs up toward the summit, opening frightful vistas of shelving cliffs and loosened crags and doubtfully balanced boulders, that chill the blood with an "if." Suddenly the walls shut together till the river flows through a cleft only thirty feet wide, its granite sides rising over 3,000 feet on either hand, and the train runs upon a bridge built lengthwise with the stream for ten rods, and suspended from steel rafters mortised into the rocks overhead. In this culminating grandeur of the Royal Gorge the traveler instinctively holds his breath, and the most garrulous are awed into reverent silence, as in the immediate presence of the omnipotent power that rent the mountains asunder. Words of description are weak and comparisons are futile to express the incomparable. Let the Eastern reader imagine Mount Washington cleft in twain by an earthquake, and a railway running through the chasm; or the Southern reader, Lookout Mountain broken apart, and cars following the course of the jagged fissure;

or let him who has looked down from Bunker Hill monument imagine himself looking up to cliffs, or down from precipices, ten times as high. But imagination is unequal to the task, for it has not entered into the mind of man to conceive the marvels wrought by the hand of the Almighty.

To him who would explore the mysteries of nature the Grand Cañon offers a revelation of the processes of world-building. The various strata of primary rock laid bare by this gigantic cleavage lie in consecutive order, distinctly revealed, as they were left when the crust of the earth was formed. Often they are bent and contorted, as if by fierce convulsions, while yet in a plastic and partially melted but tenacious mass.

The whole length of the Grand Cañon is about eight miles, and the deepest portion, known as the Royal Gorge, may be said to extend half that distance. The tourist who can spare the time will find himself richly repaid for the labor of walking through it leisurely from end to end, enjoying its grandeur and studying its manifold wonders; and if he would experience a sensation the most thrilling of his life, let him ride around to the summit, and look down upon a passing train, so far, far below that it is dwarfed by distance to the dimensions of a child's toy. Haply he will meet in the town or along the railway some person who can picture to him the manner in which the road was built: how, at some of the construction camps, men and tools, and mules and carts, were let down over the precipices by ropes, and men and animals received their food, like Elijah, from above, till they cut a track through the granite cliffs along the river; how the surveyors first picked their way through the cañon on the ice, where before only fishes and birds had been; how the rockmen hung suspended in the air, and drilled holes in the granite for blasts that sent tons of rock crashing into the stream with a noise louder than thunder; and hearing the wonderful tale he will find himself quoting the familiar adage " Verily truth is stranger than fiction."

THE UPPER ARKANSAS VALLEY.

The first station after passing the Royal Gorge is Currant Creek, ten miles from Cañon City; next comes Spike Buck, six miles farther west, neither being places of business importance; then Texas Creek, nine miles from Spike Buck and twenty-five miles from Cañon City, at the mouth of Texas Creek, a beautiful stream flowing from the Wet Mountain Valley. Nine miles further west is Vallie, and eight miles beyond, Badger, both unimportant stations.

The source of Badger Creek, opening into the Arkansas at this point, is worthy of passing notice. The stream rises in the rim of the South Park, in a very rugged and inaccessible country, west of Black Mountain. Here, at its head, a number of warm springs, highly charged with saline material, produce in a short distance a good-sized stream. Within this tepid water a jointed moss grows luxuriantly, and forms great masses of intensely green foliage just below the surface. As the water cools the saline matter is deposited upon the moss, and the moss, in an incredibly short time, is converted into a porous stone, beautiful in structure, and sold throughout the state as a natural curiosity, the exact locality where found, however, being carefully kept secret by the venders of such wares. The constant formation and petrifaction of this moss for ages has produced cliffs and waterfalls for some miles along the stream. Here trout in winter congregate in vast numbers, and are often slaughtered wholesale by the poacher, who blows them up with dynamite and transports them in a frozen state to market.

CLORA,

two miles from South Arkansas, was once a town of high promise and great aspirations, but since the construction of the railway is overshadowed by its more fortunate rival.

SOUTH ARKANSAS

is situated forty-six miles west of Cañon City, and two hundred and seventeen miles from Denver, at the point where the South Arkansas flows into the Arkansas river, and at the junction of the Leadville and Gunnison Divisions of the Denver and Rio Grande Railway. It lies at the north side of the Arkansas Valley, which here spreads out into a broad and magnificent park, affording rich pasture lands and fertile farms, smooth as a floor in places, and again rising in billowy undulations to the northwest, where long, sweeping, shingly hills stretch across the valley — the moraines left by vast glaciers that once descended from the Alpine peaks that tower so grandly beyond. The town itself nestles close to the pine-covered foothills of the mountain range known as the Arkansas Hills, which separates the valley from the great South Park to the north. It is a busy, prosperous place, having a newspaper, bank, numerous good business houses, a large stone depot, and railway warehouses. Gray's hotel is a fine two-story building, and affords superior accommodations for tourists and health-seekers.

It would be invidious to pass South Arkansas without a reference to the scenery. It commands a noble view of two of the grandest ranges of the Rocky Mountains: the Sangre de Cristo and Saguache; the former stretching to the southward, a long line of serrated peaks, the latter bearing away to the northwest, a succession of lofty summits, many of which are over 14,000 feet high. Nearest is Mount Ouray, a hoary giant, whose rounded cap has an individuality that clings to the memory, and will perpetuate the name of the great Ute chieftain to the end of time; next westward Mount Shavano, standing out from a group of snow-clad peaks, and towering above them all. Beyond are many more that will be named in our description of the upper valley. Five and one-half miles southwest of South Arkansas, and reached by a fine carriage road, as well as by the railway, is the village of Poncho Springs, near the celebrated hot springs of that name.

BROWN'S CAÑON.

Just west of South Arkansas the railway enters Brown's Cañon, a devious gorge cut through the rocky foot-hills by the Arkansas river. Sufficient in itself to make a world-wide reputation as a scenic line for any Eastern railway, it is hardly noticed by the traveler who has just passed through the greater marvels of the Royal Gorge. But it is a grand and beautiful cañon, full of interesting features to those who watch from the car-windows its tortuous curves, great heaps of loose rocks piled up higher

SILVER ORE AND BULLION.

than church steeples, enormous boulders that have fallen from the heights above and lie lazily in the gorge, changing the course of the stream that dashes itself to foam and spray as it cuts new channels around them. The railway follows the east bank of the stream, close under the mountain side; now under an overhanging cliff that makes the beholder shudder, anon opening rugged vistas upward along stern, black, forbidding gorges, lined with great shattered rocks that seem to lie dangerously insecure hundreds of feet above the track. Again, on the other side, great boulders are heaped in such fantastic shape as to suggest that the Titans may have made a western tour some time, and paused here for a play-spell. They certainly might feel at home here, if anywhere. Imagine a Titan standing astride the Royal Gorge, for instance! The Colossus of Rhodes would be a toy in comparison. Ships could pass under that; but here the dome of St. Peter's would not reach half-way to the giant's feet, and the Alleghany Mountains might pass in review under him if the gorge were not so narrow!

NATHROP.

Passing the small station called Brown's Cañon, twelve miles beyond South Arkansas, we come to Nathrop, the junction of the Alpine Branch with the Leadville Division. It is situated in Cottonwood Park, at an altitude of 7,500 feet, and is surrounded by a promising mineral district that is now being thoroughly prospected. At the time this is written Nathrop has some 300 inhabitants, a number of substantial business houses, and a large hotel. The distance from Nathrop to Alpine is eleven miles, and to Buena Vista seven and one-half miles.

BUENA VISTA,

lying thirty-seven miles from Leadville, in the beautiful Cottonwood Park, where Cottonwood Creek empties into the Arkansas, is at the junction of the Denver and Rio Grande Railway with the South Park Division of the Union Pacific. It dates its existence as a town no farther back than October, 1879, but has made such use of its opportunities that it is already a place of over 2,000 population, with substantial brick blocks, banks, public schools, churches, newspapers, and all the accessories of a prosperous western town. While a temporary railway terminus, before the Denver and Rio Grande Railway was completed to Leadville, Buena Vista was one of the liveliest camps in the Rocky Mountains — we may safely say the headquarters of the greatest stage and freighting business in the country. From fifteen to twenty-five stages a day ran to Leadville. The whole distance was an almost continuous line of teams and wagons, interspersed with pedestrians, who were generally classed as tramps, but were often as good as those who rode, and who really had the best of it, in escaping from the dust, which was so thick, so penetrating, so perpetual, that it is doubtful if its parallel ever was seen upon the continent. Those were palmy days for the new camp. Stores and warehouses, both frame and brick, sprang up by the score, and were occupied before the roofs were on. Tents by the hundred dotted the banks of the streams for nearly a mile. Thousands of horses and mules were picketed out on the park or gathered in corrals, and freight wagons were parked on every hand in numbers sufficient for an army corps in the field. When the railway passed on to Leadville there was a change. The Leadville freighters folded their tents and disappeared, and most of the dance-houses and gamblers followed, leaving the permanent residents to restore civic decorum and try to grasp the real and abiding capabilities of the town, which have proved sufficient to insure it a place among the most important of the upper Arkansas. From Buena Vista there is a toll-road to the west over Cottonwood Pass, leading to the Tin Cup district, and to Independence and Aspen. It has been one of the principal gateways to the Gunnison, but lost that character with the extension of a railway over the range. The pass is sixteen miles distant, at the head of Cottonwood Creek, the road crossing the range just above timber line, at an altitude of nearly 13,000 feet.

Buena Vista, as applied to the landscape seen from the town, is a well-chosen name. To the westward lies Cottonwood Park, a most beautiful expanse of prairie, traversed by the timber-fringed Cottonwood, and by belts of pine, that look like cultivated hedges as seen from a distance, but which may be a mile in width when once reached; for nowhere are distances more deceptive. Beyond this is a background of mountains of the first magnitude, peers of the most exalted peaks of North America, broad, firm-rooted, massive, furrowed by ancient glaciers, and seared by yet more ancient volcanoes. The nearest opposite the town are Mount Harvard, Mount Yale and Mount Princeton — monuments to the fame of the institutions after which they were named.

COTTONWOOD SPRINGS.

Six miles west of Buena Vista, at the foot of Mount Princeton, are the Cottonwood Hot Springs, where a beautiful hotel has been erected, and fine grounds laid out and improved. The location is one of the most picturesque in the entire valley, the hotel having been built in a small cove, shaded by a natural grove, and lying almost under a great cliff of white granite that rises hundreds of feet above the crystal stream that goes leaping and dancing past over its bed of snow-white pebbles. The streams in the vicinity abound with trout; the mountains invite the enterprise of those who care to climb, and interesting walks and drives may be found along Cottonwood Creek and up the cañon, in the mouth of which the springs are situated.

Passing north from Buena Vista the first station is Boulder Siding, one mile; next Riverside, seven and one-half miles; Pine Creek, thirteen and one-half.

GRANITE,

formerly the county-seat of Lake county, and later of Chaffee, but deposed by Buena Vista, is a small hamlet lying along a single street that was originally the stage road, in a narrow cañon through which the railway follows close along the river. Its name was doubtless derived from the granite walls of the cañon, that consist of heaped-up masses of huge boulders.

TWIN LAKES

is the next station north of Granite, and the place of debarkation for the lakes of that name. Carriages from the lakes connect with all passenger trains during the summer months, the distance being about four miles, over a good road.

Of all the health and pleasure resorts of the upper Arkansas Valley the Twin Lakes are perhaps the most noted. Water is nowhere too plentiful in Colorado, the largest rivers being usually narrow and rapid streams, that seldom form an important feature in the extended landscapes, and these lakes are all the more prized for constituting an exception. They are fourteen miles south of Leadville. The larger of the two lakes is two and one-half miles in length by one and one half in width, and the other about half that size. The greatest depth is seventy-five feet. These lakes possess peculiar merits as a place of resort. Lying at an altitude of 9,357 feet, — over one and three-fourths miles, — at the mouth of a cañon, in a little nook, surrounded by lofty mountains, from whose never-failing snows their waters are fed, their seclusion invites the tired denizens of dusty cities to fly from debilitating heat and the turmoil of traffic to a quiet haven where Jack Frost makes himself at home in July and August. On the lakes are numerous sail and row-boats, and fishing tackle can always be obtained. Both lakes are well stocked with fish, and the neighboring streams also abound in mountain trout. Surrounding the lakes are large forests of pine, that add their characteristic odor to the air. The nearest mountains, whose forms are reflected in the placid waters, are Mount Elbert, 14,351 feet in height, La Plata, 14,311, — each higher than Pike's Peak, — Lake Mountain, and the Twin Peaks. Right royal neighbors are these. And across the narrow Arkansas valley rises Mount Sheridan, far above timber-line, flanked by the hoary summits of the Park range. Several rich mining districts are being opened up in the near vicinity of Twin Lakes, that promise to give no little business importance to the locality, and build up a prosperous town. The hotel and boarding-house accommodations are good, and will be rapidly extended. During the summer months there is an almost constant round of church and society picnics and private pleasure parties coming down to the lakes from Leadville, so that nearly every day brings a fresh influx of visitors, enlivening the resort, and dispelling all tendency to monotony. Twin Lakes is the highest of all the popular Rocky Mountain resorts, and furnishes an unfailing antidote for hot weather. Even in midsummer flannels are necessary articles of apparel, and thick woolen blankets indispensable at night. The latter part of July and a part of August constitute the rainy season, when there is usually a shower every day, preceded and succeeded immediately by a clear sky and bright sunshine. The waters are always too cool for bathing, except in the case of robust people. The temperature of the lakes suggests their origin, for they are undoubtedly the result of immense glaciers that once reached from the cañons and gorges of the neighboring peaks far down the valley, carrying vast quantities of broken and disintegrated rock, and depositing it in long moraines, that constitute the hills which now, with their covering of pines, interpose to isolate the lakes from

TWIN LAKES, NEAR LEADVILLE.

the narrow meadows along the Arkansas. To the student of geology these evidences of glacial action afford an unfailing source of interest. Prof. Hayden, in his report of the United States geological survey of Colorado, devotes several pages, illustrated by maps and charts, to a description of the moraines in this vicinity. Although the glaciers have long since melted away, it is not uncommon in climbing among the mountain gorges, late in summer, to find great masses of snow, resulting from avalanches that came down from the mountain sides during the winter and spring. In consequence of the altitude, and the extremely rarefied air, those afflicted with consumption or heart disease should not venture to visit the lakes before securing competent medical advice. But to all not thus incapacitated Twin Lakes will prove a healthful resort in summer, and a by no means unpleasant place of residence during the entire year. Many who have wintered there prefer the climate to that of the plains; and for those whose business lies in the mountains near at hand it is undoubtedly a good place to live.

The first station on the railway, above Twin Lakes, is Hayden's, an unimportant village, and eight miles beyond is reached

MALTA,

which may be called a suburb of Leadville, being five and one-half miles distant by rail, and three by wagon road. The excessive distance by railway between the two points is necessitated by the difference in altitude. The first smelter in Lake county was erected at Malta in 1875, three years before Leadville came into existence. Malta has aspirations, and is not without considerable basis therefor. It is the junction of the Leadville Division of the Denver and Rio Grande Railway, with its Blue and Eagle River Branches, and must naturally become a distributing point of some consequence.

LEADVILLE.

Proudly pre-eminent among the mining towns of the United States stands the city of Leadville. No other city can boast of so marvelous a growth under such adverse circumstances. To the stranger who visits it for the first time, riding in a Pullman or reclining-chair car up to a large depot, thronged with hundreds of people, and flanked by side-tracks covered with long trains of freight cars, and who rides in a fine carriage or four-horse omnibus over paved streets, lined with solid brick blocks, past large churches and costly public buildings, to a first-class hotel, its history sounds like the wildest romance. Here he finds a city that on the 1st of June, 1880, had 15,185 inhabitants, not counting the thousands of miners and prospectors whose cabins dot the neighboring mountains, and who as fully belong to Leadville as those who actually find a domicile in it, and which has been steadily growing ever since; a city with Holly waterworks, gas works, an extended telephone system, an efficient fire department uniformed and drilled, a uniformed police force, several military companies, and a large number of prosperous and well-constituted civic and secret societies. He finds, further, three large daily newspapers, comparing favorably in size, amount of matter published, dignity and ability, with the best newspapers in cities of 100,000 inhabitants at the East, yet well supported and paying large dividends to the proprietors; and he must, perforce, believe that he is in the midst of an educated community pervaded with intense intellectual activity. He finds six fine church buildings, and eight religious organizations, paying salaries of $2,000 a year and upward to their ministers, and is sure that at least a few of the salt of the earth are gathered here to leaven the mass of devotees at the shrines of Mammon set up amid the sandy gulches and beds of grimy ore. He finds a stately brick court-house, and knows that Justice balances her scales over the fierce struggle for wealth that has wrought all these marvels. He finds a grand opera house that cost $78,000, and knows that fashion has kept pace with wealth. He finds a large and well-appointed public hospital, and feels that the glitter of gold and silver has not blinded the eyes of Charity. He finds a thorough system of public schools, and a high-school building that cost over $40,000, and is surprised more than ever. He finds five banking establishments, and learns that one of them alone received $31,000,000 in deposits during the year 1880. He is shown ten large smelting establishments running thirty furnaces, also three stamp mills, amalgamating works, extensive sampling works, and other works for handling ore, costing in the aggregate millions of dollars, and shipping during the year 1880 $15,750,000 worth of ore and bullion, or over $1,000 to every soul in the place, as shown by the census. He looks around him and sees no lack of any of the appliances of the most advanced civilization at the marvelous height of 10,139 feet above sea level.

Such is the Leadville of to-day. Revert backward to a description of the same spot as it existed in 1877. Far up among the mountains, two miles above the sea, was a narrow gulch lined with sage brush, and bordered by sloping hills that, followed upward a few miles, proved to be benches of the mountain chain rising above timber line into the region of perpetual snow. Three miles below, the little rill that gurgled through the gulch emptied into the Arkansas river, itself no more than a good-sized trout brook, finding its source in the mountains ten or twelve miles above. About the gulch there were a few cabins, and in the mountains near its source a few dozens of prospectors, a little elated by the recent discovery of "carbonates." There also lingered about the gulch reminiscences of a lively camp of gold-diggers that had existed there seventeen years previous. But the isolation of the place was extreme; and its altitude was against it, for at that elevation frost came every month in the year, and gardens were an impossibility. It was a lonely, desolate spot, more than a hundred miles from the railway, and farther yet from any city, in the remote recesses of the Rocky Mountains, far up the slope of one of the highest ranges, frowned upon from the other side by Mount

Massive, one of the largest, most rugged and lofty mountains in the continental divide, on whose sides thousands of acres of snow linger till August.
The roads or trails leading to it were difficult and often dangerous, crossing some of the highest passes in the mountains above timber line, where
fierce snow-storms frequently occur in July and August.

Presto, change! A few of the great carbonate mines were developed,
and soon the long, tedious roads leading down to the plains were lined
with a living tide of men and teams in a mad rush for the " Carbonate
Camp." Through dust and through snow, down in deep cañons and high
up among the crags, they paused not till the " Magic City " was won. No
matter if hay was $200 a ton, and oats thirty cents a pound, teaming must
go on, and the eager thousands must be fed. Wealth seemed to leap from
the ground, and prices were almost fabulous. Bootblacks got twenty-five
cents a shine, and barbers fifty cents a shave, and either made from ten to
twenty dollars a day. Saloon-keepers charged twenty-five cents a drink
for cheap whisky, and grew rich in a few months. The rent of a log
shanty on Chestnut street was several hundred dollars per month. New
and better buildings were erected as fast as possible, the streets were improved, and the camp one day found itself a city. It is a notable fact that
the Leadville of to-day, great and marvelous as it is when we consider the
brief space of time in which it was built, was practially constructed while
everything had to be freighted there in wagons.

Meantime the railways were employing thousands of men in a race for
the new Eldorado; and up the long valley of the Arkansas, and down deep
in the awful cleft of the Royal Gorge, the mountains reverberated with the
blasts of gunpowder, as the track-builders cut their way through the rocks.
In July, 1880, the Denver and Rio Grande Railway was completed to Leadville, and the isolated camp beside the forsaken gulch became a near
neighbor of the cities of the plains. To those interested in railway mat-
ters the manner in which Leadville is supplied with railway facilities is
worthy of notice. A difficult approach is ingeniously overcome, and the
line is so located as to supply an independent branch track to nearly every
one of the many smelters in and around the town.

The rush is now over, and Leadville seems to be entering upon a career
of steady and abounding prosperity. The yield of bullion for 1881 will
exceed that of any previous year, while the cost of mining it will be greatly
reduced. The tourist who wishes to see something of mining and mining
processes will find in Leadville the most productive mines in the world.
Whoever would understand Colorado must go through the Grand Cañon
to Leadville, thus in one trip visiting the grandest of gorges and the greatest of mining cities.

LOCALITIES NEAR LEADVILLE.

The object of prime interest at Leadville is the mines. California
Gulch, once so famous for its placers, still yields considerable quantities

of gold dust, and is worked within the limits of the city. Fryer Hill and Carbonate Hill both rise from the suburbs of the town, and are practically located in it. On these are many of the most famous mines, easily reached by good carriage-roads. On the sides of Fryer Hill are Stray Horse Gulch and Big Evans Gulch. California Gulch runs up to the southeast, past Oro City (near which are several productive gold mines), about three miles from Leadville. South of California Gulch is Iowa Gulch, starting seven or eight miles from Leadville, at the foot of Mount Sheridan. Near this gulch are many valuable mines, and much fine scenery. To the north-west, above Malta, is Tennessee Park, a broad expanse of beautiful meadow land, bordered by pine forests that rise up to timber line on the mountain slopes. West of the city, at the foot of Mount Massive, reached by an excellent carriage-road, are fine soda springs, of great repute with all who have tried the waters. The scenery viewed from these springs is magnificent. To the east the landscape embraces Leadville, Mosquito Pass, and the famous gulches leading up into the mountains whose desolate summits stand in bold relief against the sky. To the south the Arkansas valley stretches away to the Sangre de Cristo range.

NEW MEXICAN CART.

NORTH OF LEADVILLE.

THAT portion of the Denver and Rio Grande Railway from Malta to Robinson and Kokomo, in the Ten-Mile district, a distance of eighteen miles, is the highest section of railway in North America. The road is built along the Arkansas river eleven miles to its source in a few small springs. Just before reaching this point the track crosses from the left to the right bank of the little brook, traversing the gulch on a trestle-bridge, and bears to the right for nearly a mile, making a sudden curve, and doubling backward around the head of the gulch. The surrounding scenery is grand and impressive; embracing the little valley or ravine sloping rapidly downward, the pine-clad benches reaching up only a few hundred feet to timber line, and above that the great bare mountain tops, seeming to invade the very heavens, and awful in their stern desolation, swept with storms, and breeding fierce avalanches, that rush down from the peaks, bearing with them rocks and trees, and often the cabins and shaft-houses of the miners. In these sublime fastnesses, over two miles above the level of the sea, issues from the rocks the tiny rill whose waters go wandering three thousand miles to the Gulf of Mexico, gathering tribute from a thousand streams till they become a navigable river, on whose surface vessels are run for seven hundred miles before the mighty Arkansas, twenty-three hundred miles from its source, merges its tide with the still vaster flood of the Mississippi. Thirteen miles from Leadville the railway crosses the summit of the range at Fremont Pass, at an altitude of 11,540 feet — higher than is reached by any other railway in North America or Europe, and only equaled by one other on the entire globe. There is a station at this point called Summit, near which is obtained a magnificent view of the Mountain of the Holy Cross.

ROBINSON.

Sixteen and one-half miles from Leadville, at the entrance of the Ten-Mile district, is a prosperous young town, the first building of which was erected in June, 1880, but which now has a large number of business houses, a good hotel, bank, newspaper, etc. Near Robinson are several very productive mines, which have occasioned its rapid growth, and promise, with the help of new discoveries and developments, to make it one of the most prosperous mining centers in the vicinity. It is also the site of extensive smelting works. Altitude 10,781 feet.

KOKOMO,

one and one-half miles beyond Robinson, was located January 8, 1879, at the same time as Carbonateville, a once flourishing but now nearly deserted town, two miles distant. To the northwest of Kokomo is Sheep Mountain, the town-site being on the extreme southeastern slope. Directly north is Elk Mountain, and to the northeast is Jack Mountain, with Tucker, Copper, and Hornish Mountains below, while on the south side of Ten-

RED CLIFF.

Mile Creek, directly opposite the town, are Gold Hill and Mayflower Mountains, in all of which are situated paying mines. The distance to Breckenridge, by trail across the mountains, is twenty-five miles, and to Frisco fifteen miles. The altitude is 10,408 feet.

RED CLIFF AND THE MOUNT OF THE HOLY CROSS.

The great discoveries of the precious metals in Colorado have done vastly more for the country than to enrich its treasury, for they have been

the prominent means of opening up to popular knowledge a wealth of natural beauty and sublimity which would otherwise have been hidden for ages, locked behind the granite gates of the mountains. No longer do Americans need to cross the Atlantic and climb the frosty sides of Mount Blanc, or gaze down the rock-riven slopes of Chamounix, to gratify the love for the grand and romantic in nature, which is implanted in every heart; for here we have loftier than Alpine peaks, whose crests shine with the eternal snows, and vales of beauty which the best of old Europe cannot surpass. Castellated rocks, moss-covered and vine-clad, well supply the place of old ruins; and if we seek the ancient of human workmanship we can find it in the cave dwellings and cliff houses of the Rio Mancos, west of Durango, and of the upper Rio Grande, which are hung like eagles' nests among the lofty crags, and which far antedate the Teutonic ruins of the middle ages. These are the relics of a once populous race, lost to history, — human fossils, whose lives can only be made up from the works they have left. Or we can hear the music of our *Lurleis* in the singing pools and eddies of our mountain streams. Among the romantic districts opened up by mineral discoveries, and made accessible to tourist travel by the bold engineering of the Denver and Rio Grande Railway, the Red Cliff camp and mining district must ever be prominent. To reach this place the railway leads north from Malta, near Leadville, through the small but beautiful Tennessee Park, and climbs the Mother Range, following the water-grade of the Tennessee fork of the Arkansas river, and crosses the pass of the same name far below the usual elevation of mountain passes in that vicinity. Instead of reaches of barren rock, the top of this pass is covered with a luxuriant growth of straight and tall pines, which have not yet suffered the ravages of the woodman's axe, and the ground is in summer carpeted with brilliant, many-hued mountain flowers, sheltered by the dense growth from storm and wind. The railway is, at the time of this writing, completed to the top of the pass, but everything required for its extension is prepared, and when the deep snows have melted under the sun of early spring, the lines of steel will follow the slopes of Eagle river on the other side of the range to the romantic village of Red Cliff, and will be completed in time for early summer travel. As we descend the slopes on the western side of the main range the mountains are more rugged and abrupt, and their steep sides are dotted with dumps from the shafts and tunnels of the prospectors probing them for mineral treasures.

Eagle river is a clear, dashing stream, which takes its rise in the mountains to the northeast, and has cut its way through every obstacle, until it crowns its achievements in the passage of the grand gorges of Battle and Homestake Mountains, just below Red Cliff. This village is located on a triangular plateau at the foot of Horn-Silver Mountain, and bounded on the east by Eagle river, and on the west by Turkey creek, which join their forces just below the town. On the western side Battle Mountain rises, with its steep slopes spotted with mining shafts; but a mile below it makes

MOUNT OF THE HOLY CROSS — NEAR GEORGETOWN, COLORADO.

a sharp turn to the west, and its lofty cliffs rise in sheer vertical height from the river's edge, and form, with the equally abrupt sides of Home-stake Mountain opposite, a weird and romantic cañon. A zigzag wagon-road climbs Battle Mountain opposite town, and then follows the slope to the west above the cliffs at a dazzling height, leading to the camps of Rock creek, and by trails to Aspen and the farther camps. The road is of easy ascent by horses, and furnishes a view of some of the finest mountain scenery of the Rockies. In front and to the southward rise at no great distance the summit of the Mount of the Holy Cross and other lofty peaks. Just opposite are the seam-gashed sides of Homestake Mountain, and far below glimpses can be caught of the white-plumed crests of the river in its stormy passage of the cañon. We know of no historical event which gave the name to Battle Mountain, but can easily conclude that its battle-scarred and rock-riven aspect inspired its name. There are few places in Colorado where the mineral formation shows out so distinctly as on this mountain. The lower portion of the cliffs are formed of great, deep strata of dolomitic limestone, while above them rise other cliffs of quartzite and porphyry. Between these are belts of iron and argentiferous galena, carbonized by chemical action from the lime, and forming great deposits of the precious and famous carbonates. These mineral strata are being diligently worked by prospectors and miners, and the camp is rapidly growing in importance and prosperity. Eastern capitalists are investing here, and additional reduction works are in process of erection. The easiest trail to the Mount of the Holy Cross is also from Red Cliff, and the wonderful discoveries of native gold and tellurides of gold made last fall in this mountain will con-tribute largely to the growth of Red Cliff. The name was given to Red Cliff from the mineral belts of the mountains, from the fact that where exposed to the air the oxygen has united chemically with the lead and iron, forming a red oxide of these metals, and coloring the cliffs with their red and brown shades. The sacred symbol which gives the name to the Mount of the Holy Cross is derived from two great and deep depressions, one vertical and one horizontal, which cross each other nearly at right angles on the bare, rocky, eastern slope of the mountain, which in winter become filled with great masses of snow. During the summer the snows around these depressions are melted away, leaving the rest naked, and the snowy emblem of human faith and hope stands gleaming in white splendor against the azure sky, as if nature were thus consecrating the mountains to her God, and reflects the sun glories of the heaven above it. One of the best views to be had of the Cross is from high points in the mountains near the head of the Arkansas river, where the Blue River Branch of the Denver and Rio Grande Railway crosses the range at Fremont Pass. The influence of these grand expressions of nature upon the minds of those who constantly stand in their presence is marked and historical. They are educators, which develop the æsthetic natures of men. Nowhere can a class of men be found with livelier or more hopeful imaginations, kindlier

sympathies, opener hospitalities, or honester lives, than mountain prospectors. Men who can live such lives and not feel these impulses are ever
dangerous to community, and experience confirms the truth of this. Moreover, few men who have ever spent any extended period of time in the
mountains can return to the Eastern plains without experiencing a continued
longing to be back again, which often in the end becomes irresistible.

THE GUNNISON DIVISION.

LEAVING the Leadville Division at South Arkansas, two hundred and seventeen miles from Denver, and forty-six from Cañon City, in the lower part of the upper Arkansas valley, the Gunnison Division of the Denver and Rio Grande Railway extends westward through Marshall Pass into the Gunnison country, on the Pacific side of the main range.

PONCHO SPRINGS.

Five and one-half miles from South Arkansas, at the junction of the Maysville Branch, lies the pleasant village and health resort of Poncho Springs. The hot mineral springs, over fifty in number, from which it derives its name, are situated one and one-half miles from the village on the side of the mountain, to the south of the entrance of the cañon that leads to Poncho Pass. A small hotel, with numerous cabins and tents for boarders, has been erected at the springs, and the proprietors propose to put up a commodious building at an early date. The temperature of the water, as it issues from the ground, is from 140° to 165° Fahr. We are not in possession of a full analysis of its mineral constituents. There are two series of these springs on either side of a ridge, which appears to be one of the numerous moraines extending into the Arkansas valley. But, as they approach near each other on the top of the ridge, they may be considered as one group. Many cures of severe cases of rheumatism, scrofula, and various blood diseases have been effected by regular bathing in these waters, and the springs promise to become among the most noted in the Rocky Mountains. There is a well-kept hotel at the village, and a number of good boarding-houses, affording every necessary comfort for invalids. Several livery establishments keep carriages and saddle-horses, enabling those who prefer to reside in the town and go to the springs for baths. Under the management of a few cultivated and public-spirited ladies a free public library of two thousand volumes has been collected, and a building erected for its accommodation. The locality also offers numerous attractions as a pleasure resort, and the South Arkansas river here affords excellent trout fishing. The scenery, as everywhere in the Arkansas valley, is notably grand and beautiful. Several of the loftiest peaks of the Rocky Mountains are in full view, among which are Mounts Ouray, Shavano, Antero, Harvard, and Princeton.

MAYSVILLE.

A branch of the Denver and Rio Grande Railway extends from Poncho Springs eight miles west to Maysville, the railway point for the Monarch mining district, which lies around the headwaters of the South Arkansas river, near the foot of Mount Ouray. Two smelters are in operation at Maysville, and there is every appearance of a rapid and substantial growth. The mines cover a large extent of territory on the different branches of the South Arkansas, which are five in number. The veins are both contact and fissure, the latter showing carbonates, and nearly all carrying a high per cent of lead. The new camp of Garfield, in this district, promises to prove one of the best in the vicinity.

KERBER CREEK.

The Kerber Creek Mining District lies in the Saguache range, in the northwestern part of San Luis Park, about nine miles in a direct line southwest of Poncho Pass. There are two towns which sprang up in 1880: Bonanza City and Sedgwick. A daily line of stages is run to the railway at Mears. The mineral found is principally silver, though some of the mines show fine assays of gold. Recent developments in this vicinity indicate the existence of very rich mineral veins, which may be sufficiently important to warrant the construction of a railway track into the district.

THE GUNNISON COUNTRY.

What is known as the Gunnison country is embraced in the county of that name lying in the western part of Colorado, about midway between the north and south boundaries. It includes the Elk Mountain region, and is drained by the Gunnison river and its numerous tributaries. The mean elevation of the parks and valleys is from 6,000 to 9,000 feet, and the mountain ranges which cover nearly the entire area are rugged and lofty. It lies west of the continental divide, and is therefore on the Pacific slope. In the western portions are numerous fertile valleys, well adapted to grazing, and capable of raising the ordinary farm products of this latitude. The area of Gunnison county exceeds that of the states of Massachusetts and Rhode Island combined, and all this section is rich in mines of gold, silver, copper, lead, coal and iron, which, like the wealth of the San Juan, have been waiting the advent of a railway to make them available. The Gunnison river takes its name from Lieut. Gunnison, of the United States army, who first explored this region, in 1853. The first prospectors entered it in 1866, but the Indians proved so troublesome that only feeble and intermittent attempts at prospecting were made until the fall of 1878, when the intense excitement over the wonderful discoveries at Leadville awakened a mining activity that overflowed into all parts of the state. The prospectors who came in 1878 did not, as a rule, remain in the country through the winter, owing to the almost total lack of supplies, but spent the winter at Leadville, or farther east, industriously spreading highly-

wrought accounts of the new district. Before spring hundreds were ready
to start over the range, and, impatient of delay, many went from Leadville
around via Alamosa and Saguache, a distance of over three hundred miles,
arriving at what is now Gunnison City in March or April. The only available route over the mountains from Leadville and the Arkansas valley was
through Cottonwood Pass, fifteen miles west from where Buena Vista now
stands, and that was blockaded with snow forty or fifty feet deep. However, sometime in May a tunnel was cut through the deepest snow drift at
the summit of the pass for a distance of about three hundred feet, and
through this tunnel poured an eager crowd of prospectors, traders, specu-
lators, and the various classes who ride on the crest of the flood in every

ELK MOUNTAINS.

mining excitement. Although many good mines were discovered, the lack
of transportation facilities, and the absence of smelters and reduction
works, together with a lack of capital on the part of the first discoverers,
soon discouraged those who were in quest of another Leadville, and dis-
pelled the excitement. During the latter part of 1879, and the season of
1880, steady progress was made in the development of the region ; and the
greatly increased facilities of travel and transportation afforded by the
Denver and Rio Grande Railway promise to occasion another "boom,"
and a great influx of people in 1881.

UTE RESERVATION.

The western two-thirds of Gunnison county has heretofore been included in the Ute reservation. The greater part of this is expected to be

opened to miners and settlers during the present year, when it is reason-
ably believed that many rich mining districts will be discovered and
occupied, and fertile valleys made available to the agriculturist and stock
raiser. In the eastern portions of the county the altitude is too great for
the successful growth of grain or vegetables, but there are extensive hay
meadows on the Tomichi and other eastern tributaries which are in themselves of great value.

ELK MOUNTAINS.

The mountain spur recognized as the Elk Mountains lies directly west
of Leadville, and is inclosed between the Gunnison river and the Roaring
Forks of Grand river. The trend of the range is northwest and southeast,
and the area embraced in the Elk Mountain region is about 2,500 square
miles. Along the northeastern base of the range are the Roaring Fork
mining camps, and at the southern base are Gothic and Crested Butte.
The streams flowing from the Elk Mountains are Castle, Maroon, Snow
Mass, Capitol, Sopris and Rock creeks, — branches of Roaring Fork, —
Taylor, Cement, Cascade, East, Slate and Anthracite creeks, and the north
fork of Gunnison river. The highest peak is Maroon Mountain, 14,000
feet, and there are twelve other mountains that rise to a height of over
12,000 feet, viz: Daly, Snow Mass, Sopris, Teocalli, White Rock, Belle-
view, Capitol, Castle, Crested Butte, Gothic, Grizzly and Italian.

GUNNISON CITY,

the point where the Gunnison Division connects with the Elk Mountain
Branch, and the Utah Division of the Denver and Rio Grande Railway, is
the county-seat of Gunnison county, and is situated in a large park, near
the triple junction of the Gunnison and Tomichi rivers, and Quartz creek.
Its location is central to the most important mining districts of Gunnison
county. To the south, east, north, and northwest, easily reached by well-
worked roads, are the mining camps of Cochetopa Creek, Ohio Creek,
Tomichi, Copper Creek, Taylor River, Washington Gulch, Rock Creek,
Irwin, or Ruby Camp, Gothic City, and Crested Butte. Until the further
extension of the road to Lake City Gunnison City will be the nearest railway station to that important mining center, and to the whole northeastern
portion of the San Juan country.

IRWIN, OR RUBY CAMP,

is located in the very heart of the Elk Mountains, at an altitude of 10,500
feet. It is watered by both Coal and Anthracite creeks, the one running
east to Slate river, and the other taking a northwest course, emptying into
the north fork of the Gunnison. These streams are fed by melting snows,
and their waters are clear as crystal. The site of the town is in a small
park basin, studded with pine and spruce trees, and it is regarded as one
of the most healthful mining camps in the state. It is connected with
Gunnison City by a toll-road up Ohio creek, a distance of twenty-eight

miles. On the first day of January, 1881, Irwin contained 529 buildings. Seven saw-mills were at work all the last winter to furnish lumber for the numerous building improvements in progress. Excellent sampling works and a twenty-stamp mill are in operation, and other and more extensive concerns will be erected during the spring and summer of 1881. The surrounding mining district embraces about eighteen square miles. The veins are large, appearing prominently on the surface; and in most instances mineral starts in the shape of greenish chlorides of silver, which a few feet lower change to ruby, brittle and native silver, with manifestations of sulphurets at greater depth.

Adjoining Irwin on the northwest, at an elevation of 200 feet above the town, and 11,700 feet above the level of the sea, lies Lake Brennand, a beautiful body of water, about sixty acres in extent, and surrounded by a thick forest of tall spruce trees which grow down to its edge.

ANTHRACITE COAL.

To the south and west of Irwin lie very large deposits of anthracite coal, which will be extensively mined immediately on the advent of the railway, and which, there are good reasons to believe, may in a short time supply enough of this fuel for the requirements of the entire state, and compete with the Pennsylvania anthracite as far east as it can be shipped with profit.

GOTHIC.

The mining camp of Gothic, one of the first established in the county, is thirty-five miles from Gunnison City by a road that follows up East river. It lies to the northeast of Irwin.

CRESTED BUTTE

lies to the east of Irwin, and twenty-six miles from Gunnison. It is connected with the former place by a good toll-road, and communication with Gunnison will be established by a branch of the Denver and Rio Grande Railway in the summer of 1881. It derives its name from the buttes or cliff-crowned mountains near it.

BITUMINOUS COAL

of an excellent quality, and in apparently inexhaustible quantities, is found around Crested Butte, and coking furnaces are already turning out a superior article of coke.

COCHETOPA.

On Cochetopa creek, southeast of Gunnison, about eighteen miles, a number of gold lodes were discovered in the summer of 1880, and a considerable camp, called Cochetopa, established.

PITKIN.

The town of Pitkin lies twenty-two miles southwest of Alpine; and is the first important point reached by the Alpine Branch after passing the tunnel through the mountains at Alpine Pass. It is thirty miles east from Gunnison City. The place was at first known as Quartzville, but afterward named Pitkin, in honor of the governor of the state.

OHIO CITY

Is a mining camp about seven miles south of Pitkin, at an elevation of 8,100 feet. It was started in May, 1880, by the discovery of some very promising lodes, mostly gold bearing.

TIN CUP DISTRICT.

The well known mining camp of Virginia City, in Gunnison county, is about seventeen miles from Alpine, and is connected with that station by a toll-road, which follows the north branch of Chalk creek to its head, and crossing the main range, or continental divide, at an altitude of over 12,000 feet, descends a branch of Willow creek to the camp, a distance of six miles. A little below the summit is a beautiful lake, nestled among the pines, its bed and shores being composed of shingly rocks, that were probably deposited by some ancient glacier. It is said to abound in fish. The locality receives its name from Tin Cup gulch, where the first gold was discovered in 1861. Some passing prospectors thought the ground looked favorable for placer operations, and one of them washed some of the sand in a tin coffee-cup, and obtained color. The district includes four groups of mines: Gold Hill, Anna Mountain, Hillerton, and American Mountain. Hillerton, a beautifully located town, two miles north of Virginia City, at the head of Taylor Park, has several good business houses, and if the neighboring mines prove remunerative, is likely to become a place of some importance. A smelter is in operation at Hillerton, and rich placer mines in the vicinity have been worked more or less every year since 1861.

ASPEN,

The county-seat of the newly created county of Pitkin, and the principal point in what is described as the Roaring Forks mining district, is located on the Roaring Fork, a tributary of Grand river, near the mouth of Castle creek. Although only forty miles from Leadville in a direct line, Aspen can only be reached from that city by a devious route of over twice that distance, via Cottonwood Pass. From Buena Vista the distance is seventy-five miles. The altitude of Aspen is 7,775 feet. A toll-road is projected to Red Cliff, which will be the most accessible railway station on the completion of the Denver and Rio Grande to that place. Another road is also in progress over the Saguache range from Twin Lakes, via Independence, a new camp near the headwaters of the Roaring Fork. Only surveyed in the spring of 1880, the growth of Aspen and the surrounding mining camps was such as to necessitate the formation of a new county the following winter. The mines around Aspen are principally contact veins, carrying a high grade of silver ore. Twelve miles from Aspen is Ashcraft, where there are several paying mines, both contact and fissure veins. At Independence there is a stamp-mill and several paying mines, principally gold.

The Roaring Fork district has wonderful attractions for sportsmen. In the parks are found immense herds of elk, and black-tailed or mule deer. Frequently hundreds of elk are found in one herd, and a good hunter may kill a score of them in a day. Bears are also common, and the waters abound with ducks and geese. Trout can be caught in vast quantities in every mountain stream.

A BURRO TRAIN IN THE SAN JUAN.

PUEBLO TO ANTONITO.

LEAVING South Pueblo, the railway takes a course a trifle to the westward of south for a distance of fifty miles to Cuchara, crossing the St. Charles river at San Carlos, and the Huerfano river at Huerfano. The valleys of the St. Charles, Huerfano and Cuchara rivers contain a considerable amount of good farming land, and furnish many valuable cattle and sheep ranches. In the two last named valleys the inhabitants are principally Mexicans, and the buildings are nearly all of adobe, in true Mexican style. This portion of the road is for the entire distance along the plains, leaving the Greenhorn Mountains to the right. The changing views of this range, and of the Spanish Peaks to the south, give constant variety to the otherwise sombre landscape, while the attention is continually occupied by the luxuriant vegetation along the streams, and the primitive and picturesque surroundings of the ranches and corrals. The clay-colored hills, and rich alluvium of the valleys, together with frequent cactus patches, give a semi-tropical appearance to the country, which is heightened by the rude Mexican dwellings. Before passing westward from Cuchara toward the San Luis Park, we will continue due south to

EL MORO,

the end of the line in this direction. El Moro is thirty-six miles south of Cuchara, on the Purgatoire river, at which point the Denver and Rio Grande Railway crosses the Atchison, Topeka and Santa Fé. El Moro derives its importance from the extensive coal mines in its vicinity, which supply a fine quality of coking coal. The mines of the Colorado Coal and Iron Company at this point, during the year 1880, produced 81,697 tons of coal, 50,000 tons of which were converted into coke. Trinidad, on the Atchison, Topeka and Santa Fé Railroad, is five miles from El Moro.

CUCHARA TO VETA PASS.

From Cuchara the railway turns westward toward Veta Pass, following up the Cuchara river. Walsenburg, the county-seat of Huerfano county, is six miles west. It is a thriving town, first settled by a colony of Germans. From this point the railway bears boldly toward the Sangre de Gristo range, which it must pass on its way to the San Juan. To the left,

in full view to their utmost summits, are the twin mountains known as the
Spanish Peaks, two isolated sharp cones, rising from the plain respectively
13,620 and 12,720 feet above sea level, their bare symmetrical tops often
hidden among the clouds.   These peaks are among the most unique land-
marks of the outlying spurs of the Rocky Mountains; and although their
symmetry and smooth outlines at first deceive the eye, which fails to per-
ceive their full magnitude, they grow upon the beholder from their first
appearance till they are lost from sight as the train winds around the far-

VETA PASS AND SIERRA BLANCA.

ther side of Dump Mountain, and form a picture that memory recalls with
pleasure long afterward.

Passing Wahatoya, the next station, seven miles beyond, Veta Mountain and Sierra Blanca appear. From here to the summit of Veta Pass
the scenery ranks with the finest on the continent.

La Veta, twenty-one miles from Cuchara, is a pleasant village in a
beautiful agricultural valley, and a place of considerable business importance.

VETA PASS

VETA PASS.

From La Veta to the top of the range it is steady climbing, the average grade for twenty-one and one-half miles being 211 feet to the mile. The road follows a mountain brook that dashes down from the heights in front, over which the railway must pass. For miles the serpentine windings of the track keep varying the relative positions of the mountains and changing their aspect. The valley deepens below, the backward horizon recedes, and the plains grow vaster, while the Spanish peaks take on grander proportions. The sensation of height, and of climbing rapidly without exertion, is inspiring. Soon the train is gliding up a beautiful ravine, the flashing cascades of the stream on the left, and, at the right, rising seemingly almost from the track; for thousands of feet, is the smooth side of Veta mountain. For a short distance up this mountain there extends a border of small pines, beyond which the ascent is abrupt and worn smooth by sliding stones. A rounded rock started near the top might roll a mile before it stopped. In front, a little to the left, is a projecting mountain with smooth sides sparsely covered with pines. Near the top is a red line that resembles a trench, so high up, yet so near at hand, that it seems impossible that the railway shall reach it. The mountain is Dump Mountain, and the seeming trench is the railway track. Few travelers can contemplate rounding that point without a slight quiver of the nerves. The train enters the narrow glen between Dump and Veta mountains, passing close under the point mentioned and a long distance beyond it, till suddenly, near the head of the gorge, the track makes an abrupt bend, the train changing direction almost as suddenly as a soldier at the command "About, face." This is the celebrated Muleshoe Curve. Passing this curve the line runs diagonally up the mountain at a grade which makes the engines labor, while the height rapidly increases till the passenger is looking almost straight down for hundreds of feet. The air is cool and electrical, and the traveler beholds with thrilling ecstasy a scene whose impress will remain while memory endures. After turning the face of the mountain, for nearly a mile the view from the platform of the rear car, embracing the valley up which the ascent has been made, the towering Spanish Peaks, the stupendous proportions of Veta mountain, and the far off, vast expanse of plains beyond them all, is one upon which it would be a delight to dwell. But the train passes steadily in its winding course along the brow of the mountain and glides into the timber, reaching the highest point at Veta Pass, where there is a fine stone station house, at an altitude of 9,339 feet.

From Veta Pass the railway courses along several ravines down the side of the range into San Luis Park: the most interesting feature of the scenery being a succession of views of the snowy peaks of Sierra Blanca, to the right of the track.

PLACER,

seven miles below Veta Pass, is a town of several hundred inhabitants, and has a good hotel, which enjoys an enviable popularity as a breakfast and supper station. There is a smelter near the town, and in the mountains a few miles distant several gold lodes have been discovered which promise to develop into valuable mines; in which event Placer will become an important mining center. From Placer the railway descends a beautiful val-

SPANISH PEAKS, FROM VETA PASS.

ley to Fort Garland, near which San Luis Park begins to unfold its panorama of mountains, buttes, mesas, and plains.

FORT GARLAND

is a military station which has long been occupied by United States troops' and has played an important part as a point from which to command the San Luis Park, and protect the settlements from Indian raids. It is not a fortified post, but merely a collection of adobe buildings, consisting of offi. cers' quarters, barracks, storehouses, stables and corrals. But a few years since it was regarded as an isolated frontier outpost. Now that the rail.

way has pushed so far beyond it the troops will doubtless be removed, and the adobe houses, deserted, go to ruins.

SIERRA BLANCA.

It is doubtful if any other railway in the world affords, in an equal distance, so fine a view of mountain and plain as that unfolded by the twenty-four miles' ride from Fort Garland to Alamosa. At the right, rising directly from the valley, the lower slopes clad in vast forests of pine, appear the

SIERRA BLANCA.

sublime heights of Sierra Blanca, its grand cluster of white granite peaks lifting into the sky their sharp pinnacles, splintered and furrowed by the hand of the Almighty. It is 14,464 feet high, or over two miles and four-fifths, and the highest mountain but one in the United States. Surely it is worth a journey across the continent to obtain such a view of such a mountain. Although a part of the range, it stands out into the park like a monarch taking precedence of a lordly retinue. Two-thirds of its height is above timber-line, bare and desolate, and, except for a month or two of the summer, dazzling white with snow, while in its abysmal gorges it holds eternal reservoirs of ice. To the north and south, in bold relief for a distance of nearly two hundred miles, it is flanked by the serrated pinnacles of the Sangre de Cristo range. Such is Sierra Blanca, and the region that owns its majestic presence is the great

SAN LUIS PARK,

which may be likened to a portion of the great plains, larger than the state of Connecticut, set in among the Rocky Mountains. There is a large extent of irrigable land in this park, only a small portion of which has

FORT GARLAND.

been improved. Wherever irrigation has been practiced the soil has responded with valuable crops. The Rio Grande alone is capable of furnisning water to irrigate a large portion of the park, and there are several other streams whose waters may be used.

ALAMOSA.

Twenty-five miles from the foot of Sierra Blanca, across the dead level of the park, lies the prosperous young city of Alamosa, on the Rio Grande river. It has about 1,000 inhabitants, and many substantial buildings. It was for a time the terminus of the San Juan division, and has built up an extensive wholesale trade. The park for many miles in every direction is nearly as level as a floor. At the south of the town are extensive and valuable meadows. During the summer of 1880 one man had eighteen mowing-machines running for himself and others, cutting 800 tons of hay on his own account.

A few miles south of Alamosa, on Conejos creek, some 200 Mormons have founded a settlement, and built two towns, called Manassa and Ephraim, about four miles apart. They do not practice polygamy, and are an industrious and prosperous people.

DEL NORTE.

Above Alamosa, forty miles distant to the northwest is Del Norte, the county-seat of Del Norte county. Its population by the census of 1880 was 825. Elevation, 7,750 feet. Del Norte is connected with Alamosa by a daily line of stages, and is on one of the most traveled routes to Silverton, Saguache, and other points in the San Juan and Gunnison countries. A branch of the Denver and Rio Grande Railway is projected from Alamosa to Del Norte, and will doubtless be completed before the close of 1881. Del Norte is situated on the Rio Grande, like Alamosa, and, like that city, commands a fine view of the mountains.

WAGON-WHEEL GAP.

Thirty miles west of Del Norte, on the stage road to Silverton, is the romantic gorge known as Wagon-wheel Gap. The Rio Grande here cuts its way through the mountains, which rise on either hand in almost perpendicular walls, the gap being so narrow that there is only room besides the river for the road, which runs closely along the brink of the stream under the cliffs. The surrounding mountains abound in the wildest and most romantic scenery. There are three springs a mile from the gap, with a hotel and bathing establishment, containing two fine plunge baths. One of the springs boils up in a basin, seven by eleven feet in size. The waters have a temperature of 150° Fahr., and are of much repute. They are purgative, being strongly impregnated with sulphate of soda, or Glauber's salt. Another spring is hot soda, very pure and pleasant to the taste, but containing too much alkali to be drank continually. Hardly ten feet from these hot springs is a spring of intensely cold water.

ANTELOPE SPRINGS

are in Antelope Park, twenty miles west of Wagon-wheel Gap. These springs differ in their mineral constituents, as also in the fact that some of them are hot and others cold.

SAGUACHE,

the county-seat of Saguache county, is thirty-three miles north and east of Del Norte, in the northern part of San Luis Park. It is of about the same size as Del Norte, and has an elevation of 7,723 feet. It is surrounded by a rich farming region. The Saguache river, and San Luis, La Garita and Carnero creeks, all flow into what are termed the San Luis Lakes, a large tract of marshy land and shallow ponds, in which the water all sinks into the ground or is evaporated, as there is no surface outlet.

Saguache county is one of the best agricultural and grazing counties in the state, producing large quantities of hay, grain and potatoes. The hay crop in 1880 aggregated 8,000 tons. Nowhere else is irrigation so simple and inexpensive; for both the Saguache and the San Luis have their channels on the uplands, and flow above the land from which their waters are drawn for irrigation. About one-fifth of the population are Mexicans. The southern portion of the San Luis Lakes reaches to within twenty miles of Alamosa. Their marshes afford unsurpassed duck shooting.

ANTONITO AND CONEJOS.

Twenty-nine miles southwest of Alamosa is Antonito, the junction of the New Mexico and San Juan Divisions. It is a lively little town, and has been a favorite resort of gamblers and roughs, and the scene of summary

CHURCH AT ESPANOLA.

executions by vigilance committees. The site of Antonito is also in the level park, surrounded by fine agricultural, grazing and meadow lands. Only a mile from Antonito is the old Mexican adobe plaza of Conejos, the county-seat of Conejos county. It contains a large Catholic church and chapel, and also a convent and academy. Those travelers for business or pleasure whose routes do not carry them farther south will find in Conejos a typical Mexican town, a visit to which will repay them for stopping over a train or a day.

ANTONITO TO SANTA FÉ.

THE New Mexico Division of the Denver & Rio Grande Railway starts from Antonito, two hundred and seventy-nine miles from Denver, and at present extends ninety-one miles to Espanola, a station on the Rio Grande river, twenty-three miles from Santa Fé, the capitol of the Territory of New Mexico. At Espanola fine Concord coaches connect with all passenger trains, and run through to Santa Fé in about four hours. In point of distance and time this is the shortest line from Denver and Pueblo to Santa Fé, and, including as it does the beautiful scenery of Veta Pass, the San Luis Park, and Comanche Cañon, must always be a popular route with tourists. Leaving Antonito, the railway speedily ascends to the mesas, or table-lands, at the foot of San Antonio mountain, and follows these mesas for a distance of about sixty-five miles, to where it descends through the Comanche Cañon to the Rio Grande, at the Mexican town of Embudo. The mountain of San Antonio, rising from the level park to an altitude of 11,000 feet, smooth and round, in the shape of an inverted shallow bowl, and seen from all portions of the park, is a striking and curious landmark. Surrounded by lava beds in all directions, it is probable that at some time it was the site of an enormous volcano. Not far from its base a circular space, several acres in extent, surrounded by a natural fence of rock a few feet in height, is known as the "natural corral." We do not know that any theory has been advanced as to its formation. From the foot of San Antonio to Comanche Cañon the railway is built over the high mesas composed entirely of lava beds, covered only by a scanty soil, which suffices for the support of no more valuable vegetation than piñons and sage brush. There are no inhabitants save the section hands and necessary employes at the few and far apart stations. Occasionally, in summer, some solitary Mexican drives in a flock of sheep that obtain a scant subsistence for a few days or weeks upon the thin grass that is hardly perceptible. Water for the stations and for the engines is transported in large tanks on flat cars by regular water trains. Several miles to the west of the railway, on the mountain slopes, there is much valuable pine timber. The station and section houses, as is the case everywhere on the line, are commodious and well constructed buildings

Notwithstanding the aridity of the soil there is much on this line to attract the tourist. In the first place he is seldom out of sight of the Sangre de Cristo mountains, one of the grandest of all the Rocky Mountain ranges, running parallel with his course at the east side of the park; and there are many far-reaching and magnificent views of the park, and beautiful glimpses of the Taos Valley. Almost everywhere the scope of vision is wide and grateful to the eye. Often the piñons, a dwarf variety of the pine, low, stunted and gnarled as they are, have been so disposed by nature as to suggest the art of the landscape gardener, and open up charming vistas through which the great meadows the distant, pine-covered foot-hills, or the snow-capped mountain summits are seen with striking effect. And

STAGE STATION IN NEW MEXICO.

the reflective mind finds material for study in the vast masses of lava which overlie the country, the trend of the mesas, and the probable origin and direction of the volcanic flow. Between the stations of Volcano and No Agua there are huge cliffs of volcanic rock exposed in such positions as to indicate the existence there of the crater of an immense volcano. Prof. Hayden speaks of the valley of the Rio Grande as one great crater, including within its rim a large number of smaller craters and dikes, out of which has been poured at some time a continuous mass of melted material. All of the valleys, small and great, give evidence that they have been worn out of this mesa.

OJO CALIENTE.

The celebrated hot springs of Ojo Caliente, New Mexico, are situated eleven miles west of Barranca, a station a few miles north of the entrance to Comanche cañon, and sixty-four miles south of Antonito. Stages to and from the springs connect with passenger trains, making quick time over an excellent road. The altitude of the springs is about 6,000 feet, and the climate at all seasons of the year mild and pleasant. The springs have been noted for their curative properties from time immemorial, having been frequented by the Indians previous to Spanish occupation, and highly esteemed by both races since that date. They have proved remarkably successful in the treatment of rheumatism, skin diseases, derangement of the kidneys and bladder, and especially of all venereal diseases. Cases of paralysis, after resisting the usual appliances of medicine, have been sent to Ojo Caliente, and immediately and permanently relieved. There are at present accommodations for upward of sixty guests, with good bathing facilities. However, work is in progress on a large hotel, with room for two hundred persons, and a first-class restaurant on the European plan is to be established early in the spring. It is also proposed to erect a number of small cottages for the use of families. The springs lie in a pleasant valley, one thousand feet lower than Barranca, surrounded by high bluffs capped with basaltic cliffs. On the top of these cliffs are table-lands on which are found the ruins of prehistoric buildings, not unlike the Indian pueblos of the present day, but of which the native Indians know nothing and even their traditions furnish no account. Four miles above the village are larger springs of tepid water, the mineral deposits from which have built up great mounds, full of strange caves and glittering with saline incrustations. About three miles from Ojo Caliente is a high mountain called Cerro Colorado, from its peculiar reddish brown color, which according to the statement of the inhabitants, exhibited marked evidences of volcanic action only fifty-four years ago. It has a well defined crater, and offers an inviting field for the investigations of the geologist. The Eureka placer mines, twenty-five miles above the springs, on the Ojo Caliente river, are attracting much attention, and may soon become the occasion of a new mining excitement. From their sheltered situation the springs are a peculiarly favorable resort during the winter months. The mountains keep off the winds; but little snow falls; almost every day is bright and sunny, and the temperature seldom falls much below the freezing point. The tract on which the springs are located is an old Spanish land grant, sold by the Spanish government ninety-three years ago to the first civilized proprietors of the watering-place.

PUEBLO OF SAN JUAN.

COMANCHE CAÑON,

by which the railway descends to the Rio Grande valley, a short distance above Embudo, is difficult, rugged and striking. Frequent cuts are made through hills of marl, overlaid with a heavy drift of basaltic rock.

Some twenty miles above Embudo, to the northeast, is the fertile and thickly populated Taos valley, about eighteen miles in extent from east to west, and about sixteen miles from north to south. All the available ground is occupied by Mexicans and Pueblo Indians. The valley is noted

PUEBLO INDIANS.

for its large production of wheat. It contains the Mexican town of San Fernandez de Taos, and the old Indian Pueblo de Taos. The latter is inhabited by about 500 of the Pueblo Indians, and is surrounded by a small reservation, which they cultivate. In the mountains north of Taos are extensive and valuable gold mines.

THE ANCIENT PUEBLOS.

The Pueblo de Taos is one of twenty-six similar Indian towns (pueblo is the Spanish for town, or village), nineteen of which are situated in New Mexico, and seven in Arizona. Nine of them are on the line of the Denver and Rio Grande Railway, or in its immediate vicinity, viz: Taos, Picurio, San Juan, Santa Clara, San Ildefonso, Pojuaque, Nambe, Cuyamanque and Tesuque.

These Indians have long been a subject of interest to the historian and the ethnologist. The Spaniards under Cortez found them much more civ-

PUEBLO POTTERY.

ilized than the nomadic tribes surrounding them, cultivating the ground for a subsistence, and residing in villages fortified as at the present time. Although most of them are attached to the Roman Catholic church, many are said to retain the old Aztec rites, and each day at sunrise ascend to the

top of their houses, expecting the long looked for coming of their Monte.
zuma.

The different pueblos closely resemble each other in construction. The
dwellings are all built of mud-colored adobes, or sun-dried bricks, and are
arranged so as to inclose a plaza, or public square. The walls are from
two to four feet in thickness, and the roofs are of timbers covered with dirt
a foot or more in depth. Many houses are two, and some even four and
five stories, or rather terraces, in height, each successive story being set
back some twelve or fifteen feet from the side walls of the next story
below. The usual manner of entering these dwellings is by ascending a
ladder outside the building to the roof, and through a hole descending to
the interior by another ladder; though some, as a very modern improve-
ment, have doors cut through the side walls. This method was doubtless
adopted as a defensive measure during troublesome times, when it was
often necessary to convert the pueblo into a fortress from which to repel
hostile invasions. Large clay ovens, shaped like the snow-houses of the

PUEBLO OF TAOS.

Esquimaux, are seen on many of the roofs, which arrangement may also
be attributed to the fortress-like character of the dwellings. They use a
clumsy cart called a "caretta," the wheels of which are cut out of solid
blocks of wood, and mounted on a very heavy axle, the tongue being
upheld by a yoke fastened to the oxen's horns, upon which the whole
strain of the draft is thrown in the absence of bows. For plows they use
sharpened sticks, drawn in the same manner. Unlike the nomadic and
warlike tribes, they are self-supporting, raising crops of corn, wheat,
pumpkins, melons, red pepper, beans, apples, plums, peaches, grapes, and
apricots. They have also large numbers of horses, mules, donkeys, cattle,
sheep, and goats.

THE PUEBLO DE TAOS,

twenty miles above Embudo, is considered the most interesting, as it certainly is the most perfect, specimen of a Pueblo Indian fortress. It consists of two communistic houses, each five stories high, and a Roman Catholic church, now in a ruined condition, which stands near, although apart from, the dwellings. Around the fortress are seven circular mounds, which at first suggest the idea of being the work of the Mound Builders. On further examination they prove to be the sweating chambers, or Turkish baths, of this curious people. The largest appears also to serve the purpose of a council chamber and mystic hall, where rites peculiar to the tribe, about which they are very reticent, are performed. The Pueblo Indians delight to adorn themselves in gay colors, and form very interesting and picturesque subjects for the artist, especially when associated with

RUINS OF TAOS CATHEDRAL.

their quaint surroundings. They are skilled in the manufacture of pottery, basket making, and bead work. They used, also, to weave all the fabrics they wore, but the blankets and pantaloons of Uncle Sam are now common articles among them. At the back of the pueblo, which stands near the foot of the mesa, and watered by the stream from which the farms are irrigated, is the sacred grove of the tribe. It is some two miles long by half a mile wide, and is the most noble collection of cottonwood trees, of a species distinct from, and intermediate between, the broad and narrow leafed varieties that the writer has ever seen. No one who has not rambled through the sacred grove of the Pueblo de Taos has any idea of how noble a tree is the often despised cottonwood.

SAN JUAN AND SANTA CLARA.

The Pueblo of San Juan, a little larger than that of Taos, is situated directly on the line of the road, across the river from Chamita; and Santa Clara is a few miles below. They afford an excellent opportunity of studying the habits of this interesting people.

SAN FERNANDEZ DE TAOS.

No little historic interest attaches to the Mexican town of San Fernandez de Taos, which was the seat of the first overland trade to the

Missouri river in 1822. Here Gov. Bent, the first civil governor under the authority of the United States, was assassinated during an insurrection in 1847, and here, also, was for many years the home of the famous hunter, scout, and officer, Col. Kit Carson, here the place of his death, and here his remains are buried.

In the vicinity of Santa Clara and San Juan are mesas the sides of which are high cliffs, often assuming stately, monumental and castellated forms. In many places the faces of the cliffs are full of caves, once occupied by the ancient cliff dwellers. These caves and cliff dwellings have been but little explored, and open an interesting field for investigation, being very numerous over a large extent of territory contiguous to the railway. These singular abodes are to be found embedded in a soft stratum of sandstone, capped and protected by a thick layer of basalt. They are so well hidden

from observation by their sameness of color that a guide is almost a necessity to find them. An enterprising pioneer who keeps the dining-room at Embuda has fitted up a number of Mexican adobe houses for the reception of visitors in the by no means uncomfortable style characteristic of the district.

From the terminus at Espanola, near the Mexican village of Santa Cruz, the traveler has a stage ride to Santa Fé, over a good though somewhat sandy road, most of the way among the novel but barren and worthless marl hills, that resemble in appearance the so-called "bad lands" of Dakota, and passing through the pueblos of Pojuaque, Cuyamanque and Tesuque.

CLIFF COTTAGE.

SANTA FÉ.

The city of Santa Fé claims the distinction of being the oldest town in the United States; a claim that is easily admitted when we consider that it was a populous Indian pueblo when the first Spaniards crossed the territory now known as New Mexico, only forty or fifty years after the discovery of the Western Continent by Columbus.

A STREET SCENE IN SANTA FE.

The first European who penetrated into this region was Alva Nuñez Cabeza de Vaca, a Spanish navigator whose vessels were wrecked somewhere on the coast of Texas in 1530, and who, with a portion of his crew, wandered for six years across the plains and mountains until he finally joined his countrymen under Cortez in Mexico. His report of the country through which he passed led to an expedition in 1539, by Marcas de Niza, a Franciscan friar, who was frightened out of the country by the Indians, and returned to Mexico with a marvelous account of the extent, population and wealth of the country, the magnificence of its cities, and the ferocity of its people.

A BURRO.

In 1539 to 1541 the famous expedition of Coronado passed through the pueblo where Santa Fé now stands, crossed the range and traversed the plains until he came to the Missouri river, at a point probably near the present site of Atchison or Leavenworth. In 1581 Friar Augustin Ruiz headed an expedition which formed a settlement at Paura, a few miles north of Albuquerque, which was subsequently broken up by the natives and Ruiz killed. Antonio Espejo came with an expedition to rescue Ruiz, and on his return attempted to visit Santa Fé, but was repulsed by "40,000 native warriors." In 1597, according to the best credited accounts, Juan de Oñate founded a colony near the junction of the Chama with the Rio Grande, in the immediate vicinity of the terminal station of Espanola. It was about this date that a Spanish settlement was formed in Santa Fé, and the church of San Miguel erected.

Pedro de Peralto was the first governor, in 1600, and lived in the same adobe " palace " that is now occupied by Governor Lew Wallace, and from which Mrs. Wallace has written many interesting letters to the Eastern press.

In 1680 there was a great rebellion of the natives, who entirely drove out the Spaniards, and obliterated as far as possible all evidences of their

THE PLAZA AT SANTA FÉ.

occupation, dismantling, among other buildings, the old church of San Miguel. Fourteen years later they were reconquered by Diego de Vargos. From that time to the present Santa Fé has had an eventful history. The Mexicans in 1821 declared their independence of Spanish rule, and after that there were numerous insurrections until the occupation of the territory by the United States, in 1846. Then came the war of the rebellion in 1861, during which Santa Fé was captured by the rebels and recaptured by the Union forces.

During all these years Santa Fé has changed its character but little, and is to-day, in general appearance, very much the same old Mexican town that is has been for nearly three hundred years. There is the same old plaza, the same adobe buildings nearly all the way around it, the same one-story adobe houses surrounding the same placitas, the same suburban fields and gardens, and the same swarthy, dark-eyed population, still speaking the musical Spanish tongue. Wood is still brought into town on the backs of donkeys, or burros, as they are called here, and by this handy conveyance can be left inside the placitas.

CHAPEL OF OUR LADY OF GUADALUPE, SANTA FÉ.

Among the objects of most interest to the stranger are the church of San Miguel, the oldest in America; the governor's palace; the ruins of old Fort Marcy, on a bluff from which is had a fine view of the town; the extensive and charming garden of Bishop Lamy; and the plaza, around which centers the life of the town.

The famous San Miguel church, though a portion of its tower has been demolished by the elements, still rears the same adobe walls that have

CHURCH AND COLLEGE OF SAN MIGUEL, SANTA FÉ.

stood for three centuries, and the interior is well preserved and in present-able shape. It has no exterior beauty and no interior magnificence, its only interest being in its age and the sacred uses for which it has been kept up during almost the entire period of civilization in America. On a great beam, as plain as if made but yesterday, is the Spanish inscription traced there one hundred and seventy years ago to the effect that " The Marquis de la Penuela erected this building, the Royal Ensign Don Augustin Flores Vergara, his servant, A.D. 1710." Original documents show that this refers to its restoration after the woodwork was burned by the rebel Indians. An oil painting of the Annunciation, on one side of the altar, bears on its back an inscription, seemingly dated A.D. 1287, leading to the belief that it is one of the oldest oil paintings in the world. By the side of the church is a two-story adobe house that tradition says was in existence when Coronado marched through the town.

But even quaint old Santa Fé has caught something of the spirit of the age, and boasts numerous American residents, cultivated society, and a few buildings not built of adobes, among which are a new hotel, costing $100,000, a large public hospital built of stone and brick, at an expense of from $70,000 to $90,000, a Methodist church, Santa Fé Academy and San Miguel College, and a few private houses and business buildings.

The headquarters of the military district of New Mexico are established at Santa Fé, Gen. Edward Hatch, colonel of the 9th cavalry, commanding. The presence of the general and his staff officers, some of whom have families, and the governor and territorial officers, with their families, serves to keep up society interest, a point of importance to many tourists, especially ladies.

The neighborhood of Santa Fé is rich in precious stones, including turquoise, bloodstone, onyx, agate, garnet and opal. The manufacture of Mexican filigree jewelry, largely carried on here, one firm employing over twenty workmen, will be found interesting. The work is done by natives, to whom the trade has been handed down by their ancestors from time immemorial. The earliest Spanish accounts of this people state that there are " no better goldsmiths in the world." The sale extends to all parts of the United States and Europe.

The old Spanish mining district of Cerrillos, near Santa Fé, is being reopened, and there is much mining activity in the vicinity

NEW MEXICAN PLOW,

ANTONITO TO THE SAN JUAN.

THE San Juan Division of the Denver and Rio Grande Railway, travers-ing the mountains from Antonito to Durango, a distance of one hundred and seventy-one miles, and crossing the Pinos-Chama summit and the continental divide at an altitude of nearly 10,000 feet, is one of the most wonderful and romantic achievements of modern railway building, and could only be justified by the permanent and abounding wealth of the San Juan country. Looking west from Antonito, the beautiful Mesas, covered with grass and groves of scattered pines, rise with terrace-like regularity till they meet the horizon, with only now and then a rocky height, that gives no token of the difficult passes the cliffs, and chasms, and awful gorges, that lie

" Beyond the blue hills' purple rim."

The ride up these mesas, for over twenty miles, is one of the most delightful imaginable. The railway mounts the heights by an easy grade, winding in labyrinthine curves among grassy knolls and parks of dark green pines and piñons, allowing the passengers to measure the elevation by the plains below, and affording a hundred different views of Sierra Blanca, the Sangre de Cristo range, and the smooth outlines of San Antonio Mountain. Climbing these mesas in a Pullman car is indeed being

" * * carried to the skies on flowery beds of ease."

At one place, which has been called "The Whiplash," the railway doubles upon itself twice, on the side of a smooth hill, making three paral-lel tracks in a distance of a little more than a stone's throw. In one of the loops, situated in a shallow ravine, is a large, neatly-painted section-house, whose inmates are to be congratulated that their work lies very near their domicile. As a brakeman remarked, " if the train does not go at too great speed, they have time to get pretty well acquainted with the passengers before it gets past." This seemingly aimless winding among the smooth hills continues for nineteen miles from the first rise, about four miles from Antonito, and is rendered necessary by the great elevation to be overcome. Fortunately the contour of the country enables the railway to make this ascent by an easy and uniform grade, and in all its turnings there is no waste labor, its course being ever " onward and upward."

LOS PINOS VALLEY.

Rounding the point of a promontory-like hill, twenty-three miles from Antonito, the traveler suddenly looks down into the deep valley of Los Pinos creek. But he has only a few brief glimpses of its surprising beauty when a precipitous ravine branches off to the north, and the track follows the brow of the hills in a tortuous detour of nearly four miles among the pines, — expensive for the railway company, but delightful to the tourist. Going up this ravine its full length, making a long curve around its head, and coming back nearly to the starting point, past the station of Boydville, and a handsome section-house near some admirable springs of clear water beyond it, the passenger finds himself on the crest of a mountain overlooking one of the most beautiful of all Rocky Mountain valleys, over a thousand feet below. The scenery for the next nine miles is unequaled by any other railway in North America. The road follows the steep mountain side just below the summit, making a great convex bend for a distance of over four miles, and then dives into a tunnel in the granite cliffs amid the culminating grandeurs of Toltec Gorge. For all this distance, at the giddy height of over 1,200 feet, the track describes the irregular contour of the mountains in a succession of short curves, cutting through projecting masses of rock, and running over high fills, made necessary by deep and ragged gorges. Before the road was built a mountain goat could scarcely have followed its present course. Along the way are scores of the monumental rocks for which Colorado is so famous, rising in fantastic columns nearly as high as the pines beside them. The engraver has made a good picture of one of these, called "Lot's Wife." One projecting point is cut through by a well-timbered tunnel. Passing the most southern point of the bend, the first glimpse of Toltec Tunnel is obtained, at a distance of about six miles by the course of the road. It appears as a small black spot in the face of the cliff, at a point where it is cut in twain by a great chasm. From here on the tunnel appears and disappears at intervals till it is reached. Soon after passing the timbered tunnel, a sharp curve takes the train into a cove among the hills, with monument-shaped rocks on one side, and fantastic castellated cliffs rising five or six hundred feet on the other. This is known as Phantom Curve. It is indeed a wild spot, with the valley so deep below, the weird, red monumental rocks around, and the tall, shelving cliffs above. At one place, near the track, there is a small cave, in which is found a beautiful light green moss. A mile beyond Phantom Curve the railway crosses the head of the ravine on a high bridge of trestle work. From this point the track runs directly toward the valley, on a line almost at right angles with it, to where it narrows into a mere fissure in the rocks at Toltec Gorge. The ledge along which it passes is really a great wall across the head of the valley or cañon, commanding a full view of it for many miles. Here the beauty and the grandeur of the scenery are beyond description. All the features of the land-

DISTANT VIEW OF TOLTEC GORGE.

scape are on a Titanic scale. The track over which the train has just passed can be seen circling the brow of the mountain for miles, a tiny, yellowish thread. Far beyond the distant heights that shut in the valley rises the round top of San Antonio mountain, while across the valley the opposite mountains rise higher and higher in vast, receding, wooded slopes. The narrow vale with its silvery stream and park-like groves of pine and aspen, among which it would be delightful to camp during the long days of summer, recalls the happy valley of Abyssinian princes. Nor is color wanting to complete the charm of the picture. The dark hue of the pines, the light green and white of the shivering aspen, and the red and gray that alternate in the cliffs, add their subtle charms to the sublime panorama. When the train approaches the end of the wall, the passengers look almost straight down to where the stream emerges in foaming cascades from the jaws of

TOLTEC GORGE.

Down! Down! How little and how much the word may mean. Gazing from some lofty church spire or from the top of one of the towers of the New York and Brooklyn bridge, more than 200 hundred feet high, who does not grow faint and pale, and feel his heart throbbing fiercely in his breast? But do you call that depth! Double that distance downward from the railway track at Toltec Gorge, and you have hardly begun the descent. The pebble you toss from your hand drops far below, and you hear it strike again and again hundreds added to hundreds of feet distant, and yet silence does not signify that it has reached the bottom. It is simply out of hearing! Double the distance again, so far that the strongest voice can scarcely make itself heard, and when that terrible gulf is passed you might still look downward upon the tallest steeple in America; for the railway track at the brink of the chasm of Toltec Gorge is over 1,100 feet above Los Pinos creek. But in a flash, in the twinkling of an eye, the scene is changed. One parting glance at the far stretching valley and its mountain barriers, one shuddering, giddy look far down the precipice among the jagged rocks, and then all is hid from view in the darkness of the tunnel. For 600 feet the way is cut through solid granite. The train emerges upon the other side of the wall on the brink of a precipice, looking directly down into the gorge, across which the opposing cliffs rise abruptly over 2,100 feet. At the most critical point, where the downward view takes in the deepest depths of the gorge, lined with crags and splintered rocks, and bouldlers as large as churches, fallen from the cliffs above, amid which the stream dashes downward in snow white cataracts, the train runs upon a solid bridge of trestle work, set in the rocks, as if it were a balcony from which to obtain the finest possible view of this most wonderful scene.

PHANTOM CURVE.

TOLTEC GORGE TO DURANGO.

Marvelous, sensational and grand as is Toltec Gorge the climax is not reached until the railway comes to the summit which separates the waters of the Pinos from those of the Chama. From Toltec Gorge to Osier, eight miles, the elevation of the track above the torrent below gradually lessens until the valley bottom is almost reached. From Osier for some miles

EASTWARD FROM TOLTEC TUNNEL.

westward the grade of the railway is greater than that of the valley, and soon carries the line up among the topmost turrets which crown the summits of the surrounding mesas.

The country here is very broken and confused, and the road clings to, and winds around, these lofty crags like a huge serpent trying to reach the

LOT'S WIFE.

sky. Suddenly, as the traveler is rapt in wonderment, and is very naturally thinking what next, and why this fantastic piece of engineering, the train glides out from among the pinnacles at the summit and commences a very rapid descent into the dense pine forests of the Tierra Amarilla, through which the tranquil Chama wends its way.

And here we would say that no Coloradan, be he never so well traveled, has ever dreamed of such forests as cover the entire country northward from the railway to the San Juan mountains. Between the Chama river and Durango the line crosses here and there—specially noteworthy for a few miles east and west of the Chama—some of the southward extensions of this vast forest, which covers a scope of country one hundred and thirty miles east and west by from twenty to forty miles north and south, Pagosa Springs lies in the center of it, twenty-five miles north of Amargo station, and a good idea of the forest is obtained while traveling to this most interesting group of thermal springs. Here the pines grow tall and straight, and of enormous size. No underbrush hides their bright, clean shafts, and curiously enough it is only in special locations that any low trees are to be found. These monarchs of the forest seem to be the last of their race, and are destined, like the Indians, very soon to disappear. From an utilitarian point of view, however, they are of immense value, for they form a vast storehouse of the finest lumber in a country poorly supplied in general with timber fit for the saw. After crossing the Chama, and still among the pines, the line passes imperceptibly from the drainage of the Atlantic to that of the Pacific—from the basin of the Chama to that of the San Juan —and as the nearest station to the Pagosa Springs is reached a few miles west of this continental divide, we will digress for a short space to describe them.

PAGOSA SPRINGS.

The village of Pagosa Springs is situated about four miles south of the base of the San Juan range of mountains, upon the immediate southeastern bank of the Rio San Juan. It consists of a cluster of dwellings, stores, and bath-houses, among which the steam of the hot springs issues in such clouds as at times to render the entire place invisible. Immediately above the town, on the opposite side of the river, rises a flat-topped, isolated hill, whose summit contains a ledge large enough to liberally accommodate the government post which has been erected there. Utilizing the pines so abundant in the neighborhood, the buildings are all built of logs. And model log-houses they are. A more picturesque military post, both as regards location and construction, could not well be conceived.

The chief interest, however, centers around the boiling springs. The largest of these is at least forty feet in diameter, and hot enough to cook an egg or scald a pig in a few minutes. Carbonic acid gas and steam bubble up in great quantities from the bottom, and keep the water always in a state of agitation. The water has the faculty of dividing the light into its component colors, producing effects very similar to those of the

TOLTEC GORGE.

opalescent glass of commerce. Around the large spring, and extending for a mile down the creek, are innumerable similar ones, many of which discharge large quantities of almost boiling water. These hot springs, being highly charged with saline material, have produced by deposition all, or nearly all, of the ground in their vicinity, and their streams meander through its cavernous structure, often disappearing and re-appearing many times before they finally discharge into the San Juan river. This spot must grow to be a great popular resort. Its bountifully wooded and mountainous surroundings enhance the interest it otherwise possesses for the traveler and health seeker, and the medicinal value of the springs claims the attention of all who can afford time to visit them.

WESTWARD AGAIN.

Returning to Amargo Station, the railway leaves El Amargo cañon, crosses an undulating park, and follows the Amargo stream for about three miles down to the Rio Navajo. It thence runs through the Navajo cañon for about eight miles, where it reaches the San Juan. The railway then descends the valley of the San Juan for about fifteen miles to the mouth of the Rio Piedra. The valley for this distance is mostly open and contains in many places some fine farming lands. From the mouth of the Rio Piedra the line accompanies the old Spanish trail across the drainage of the country to the Rio de Los Pinos, twenty-four miles, leaving the pine forests some ten miles to the northward. Between the Rio de Los Pinos and the Animas river, another twenty-five miles, only one important stream is crossed by the road,— the Rio Florida,— upon which are to be found the ruins of some ancient pueblos, only a few miles south of the line. The point where the railway strikes the Animas is about four miles south of Durango, close to where the huge coal fields of the Animas have been opened and worked. The ruins of the Animas extend on both sides of the valley for many miles, and prove that at one time this large and fertile valley was very populous, and that the people whose buildings now form huge mounds of earth and stone had reached a very high state of civilization. The most northerly of these ruins are about thirty miles below where the railway reaches the Animas Valley.

The new military post, now known as New Fort Lewis, is situated on the La Plata, nine miles from Durango, and six miles below Parrott City, on the Parrott City and Rico road.

Parrott City is at present the county seat of La Plata county, and is the center of an active mining district.

DURANGO.

When the Denver & Rio Grande railway was located across the mountains into the San Juan country it became necessary to select a temporary terminus at a point which would best accommodate the various mining districts of that extensive region. This location was found on the Animas

TOLTEC TUNNEL.

river, three miles below Animas City, and in September, 1880, the town plat was surveyed and lots offered for sale. Since then, notwithstanding a severe winter and deep snow, it has grown with a rapidity befitting the prospective metropolis of the great mining country with which its name is already synonymous. The former town of Animas City soon found itself virtually deserted, what little business it had being absorbed by Durango. The new city is near the southwest corner of Colorado, not far from the New Mexico line, in La Plata county. It lies at an altitude of 6,500, in the beautiful and fertile Animas Valley, which is here over a mile in width. The ground rises in gentle mesas back to the superb bluffs that tower far above the valley, whose rugged and fantastic outlines are a striking feature of the landscape. Many large buildings are in process of erection or under contract, among which is a hotel block, of stone, which will be one of the largest and finest in the state. A large smelter is almost completed, and will be in full blast by June of this year.

Near Durango are extensive coal fields, underlying an area estimated at about twenty-five by sixty miles. On the outskirts of the town a bed has been opened that is thirty-two feet in thickness. The town company propose to erect water and gas works early in the season, and innumerable coaking ovens are to be constructed just below the village. It is probable that other smelters will be erected during the spring and summer, as its location and railway advantages seem to render it the most convenient center for the treatment of ores from all parts of the San Juan region. During the ensuing season Durango promises to be the liveliest place in America, and those who wish to witness or take part in the marvelous growth of a typical mining camp and railway terminus combined, in the most remote and romantic portion of the Rocky Mountains, will find what they seek at Durango.

Distances from Durango to the principal towns in the San Juan are as follows: Parrott City, twenty miles; Rico, forty-five; Lake City, eighty-five; Silverton, forty-five; Ouray, eighty-five; Junction Creek, seventeen; San Miguel, eighty-five; Ophir, sixty-five; Animas Forks, sixty-three; Howardsville, fifty-five; and Eureka, fifty-five.

Daily lines of stages are run between Durango and Silverton, Cascade, Chicago Basin, Fort Lewis, and Parrott City, and a semi-weekly line to Farmington, New Mexico. A route will be established to Rico, via a new road now under construction, at an early date.

THE SILVERTON BRANCH

Of the Denver & Rio Grande railway, extending forty-five miles due north from Durango, is being constructed for much of the distance through Animas cañon. The lower portion of this cañon is so narrow and tortuous that the line is restricted to the brink of the gorge for about eight miles, thence gradually swinging down into it. The difficulties of locating this section of road are portrayed in our engraving, where a close examination

TOLTEC GORGE ABOVE THE TUNNEL.

will reveal the engineers suspended by ropes, in a manner similar to that employed in the Royal Gorge. The scenic features of this link are not excelled by any portion of this most marvelous railway. Indeed it promises attractions so novel and striking as to establish it as a fitting climax to what may be aptly likened to a beautifully rounded poem.

THE SAN JUAN COUNTRY

embraces a mountainous region in the extreme southwestern part of Colorado, over 10,000 square miles in extent, or larger than several of the New England States combined. It comprises the counties of La Plata, Ouray, Dolores, San Juan, and Hinsdale, and a portion of Conejos, although a larger territory is frequently included in the general term. Nowhere in North America are the mountains more grand and picturesque; many of the towering peaks reaching an altitude of over 14,000 feet, rising in sharp, cone-shaped spires, that are the delight of the landscape painter. The parks are generally small, the valleys narrow, and the cañons deep and rugged. The average altitude of the parks is 8,400 feet, or over a mile and a half, while the principal towns, with the exception of Durango, are situated at elevations ranging from 8,550 feet, at Lake City, to 11,200 feet, at Animas Forks. The mountain passes by which many of the mining districts are reached are lofty and difficult, and in winter and spring obstructed by a great body of snow. The configuration of the surface is said to bear an intimate resemblance to that of the region surrounding the celebrated silver mines of Potosi, in South America. These difficult and rugged surroundings have retarded the development of the San Juan mines, and it is a remarkable commentary upon their abounding wealth, when they could only be reached by a stage journey of two to three hundred miles, and when all their supplies came in, and all their products were sent out, over this long and tedious road, that they should attract such general attention, and attain such wide celebrity.

The mines of San Juan—the Silver San Juan, as it has appropriately been called—are fissure-veins, easily found and readily traced, but like all fissure-veins requiring capital, machinery, and time, for their development. Gray copper and black sulphurets are found in all the principal lodes, and frequently rich streaks of ruby silver, tellurium, sylvanite, calarerita, and chloride of silver. Most of the ores are smelting ores.

The principal towns are Lake City, Silverton, Parrot, Ouray, Rico, and Durango.

The parks and valleys of all this region abound in game, and the streams are full of speckled trout.

SILVERTON

lies in Baker's Park, which is perfectly level, and not exceeding 1,500 acres in extent, at an altitude of 9,780 feet. Into this park flow Cement, Mineral, and Cunningham creeks, names well known to miners. Around the park rise abruptly magnificent mountains on every side, making Silverton more beautiful probably than any mountain town in Switzerland.   At the south end of the park the various streams forming the Animas river escape through the Grand Cañon of the Animas, which gorge has the mountain sides themselves for its walls.   A wagon road has been built through it for twenty miles at great expense.

Fifteen miles above Durango the Animas emerges from the cañon. Here commences a very fertile agricultural valley, which is well settled, and, situated as it is in close proximity to such an extensive mining country, it has made large fortunes for the settlers, the result of which may be seen by the character of their improvements.

North of Silverton the mountains of the San Juan are so abrupt and lofty that until the present time all produce of the mines has been transported by jacks over the range, and mining machinery has been brought in with the utmost difficulty.   The cost of transportation can best be appreciated when it is stated that the average price of hay at Silverton has been from $100 to $200 per ton every winter for many years.   Mining that could be carried on under such disadvantages must certainly prove remunerative when the advent of a railway makes such a condition of affairs a thing of the past.

LAKE CITY,

the county-seat of Hinsdale county, and a place of about 1,000 inhabitants, is located an the junction of Henson creek with the Lake Fork of the Gunnison river, fifty-five miles southwest of Gunnison City, and eighty-five miles northeast of Durango.   The first building was erected less than seven years since, and the growth has been regular and substantial.   It is in one of the most beautiful parks in the San Juan country, and the surrounding scenery is exceedingly beautiful.   Looking northeast for a distance of sixteen miles the mountains seem an impassable barrier, penetrating the very heavens.   On all sides the snowy summits tower above the city and the little basin in which it is situated.   From the south the Lake Fork of the Gunnison plunges into the basin at Granite Falls, over a precipice seventy-eight feet in height.   On the west, the waters of Henson creek having fretted their way downward in a succession of rapids, cascades and cataracts, falling 2,500 feet in sixteen miles, and breaking through a mountain barrier 2,000 feet high, flow tranquilly into the park.

Lake City has three establishments for the reduction of ores, two newspapers, a bank, and several important business houses.   As showing the extent of business transacted, the total amount of freightage paid for freight received at Lake City during the last six months of 1880 is stated at $502,787; this item alone exceeding the entire business transactions of many prosperous Eastern towns of equal population.   A large number of important mines are within a radius of less than three miles from the town. Nine miles southwest of Lake City is the flourishing camp of Capital City. Cimarron Camp is eighteen miles northwest of Lake City.

Although commonly spoken of in connection with the San Juan country, with which section we have here grouped it, Lake City will hereafter be in close business relations with Gunnison City, and best reached via that point.

RICO,

the county-seat of the newly constituted county of Dolores, which has been formed from portions of the former territory of Ouray and La Plata counties, is forty-five miles northwest from Durango, on the Dolores river. The town, as well as the intense mining activity of the region surrounding it, known as the Dolores district, only dates back to the summer of 1879. But it already boasts a city and county government, bank, newspaper, and all the accessories of municipal existence. The mines are near the town, on Telescope, Dolores, and Expectation mountains, and Horse Gulch.

LOCATING THE LINE, ANIMAS CAÑON.

OURAY,

the county seat of Ouray county, is twenty-five miles north of Silverton, and eigthy-five miles from Durango. It is a town of over 1,000 population, and the center of great mining and business industry. Situated on the Uncompahgre river, in a deep recess of the mountains, just above a series of fertile parks, its scenic attractions can hardly be surpassed by those of any town in Europe or America. Massive mountains rise all about it, seemingly almost perpendicular to the skies, and the stream flows through a cañon hundreds of feet in depth. One mile from Ouray is the so-called " Mineral Farm " of forty acres, two-thirds of which is covered with several feet of rich silver ore. At the base of the mountains are numerous hot springs, which flow around and through the town, and at the head of Uncompahgre Park, twelve miles below Ouray, on the " Four Mile Strip," is a hot spring twenty-five feet deep and 100 feet in circumference.

BAKER'S PARK AND SILVERTON.

About a mile west of Ouray, up Cañon Creek, is a cave well worth visiting. It is in a perpendicular cliff, and is reached by an entrance nearly on a level with the creek. This entrance runs back into the cliff at right angles to the stream about twenty-five feet, the roof gradually increasing in height to some twenty feet. Back of this, reached by an ascent through a narrow opening, is a chamber described as 270 feet in length, twenty to seventy feet wide and nearly 100 feet high. The sides and roof are coated with a deposit that glistens in the light, and in one corner is a petrified waterfall — a remarkable collection of stalagmites.

PARROTT CITY,

the county seat of La Plata county, lies about fifteen miles west from Durango, surrounded by valuable mines.

ANIMAS FORKS.

The mining camp of Animas Forks is situated at the confluence of the north and west forks of the Animas river, thirteen miles northeast of Silverton, and twenty-one miles southwest of Lake city, at an altitude of 11,200 feet. It is too high for a pleasant winter residence, but during the summer is a lively and productive camp.

HOWARDSVILLE,

five miles from Silverton, is one of the oldest camps in the San Juan. It is a neat little village, pleasantly located in a park at the junction of Cunningham gulch and the Animas river, at an altitude of 9,700 feet.

MINOR POINTS.

Mineral City lies midway between Silverton and Lake City, at an altitude of 11,500 feet. Above Lake City on Hensen creek, is Rose's Cabin, which is developing into a prosperous camp. Eureka, nine miles from Silverton, is the site of reduction works. Ophir is thirteen miles from Silverton.

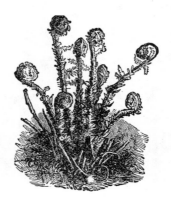

THE CLIFF DWELLINGS.

ANCIENT RUINS IN SOUTHWESTERN COLORADO.

ONE of the most interesting regions opened to tourists by the recent extensions of the Denver and Rio Grande Railway is that occupied by the famous cliff dwellings, in southwestern Colorado, and the adjacent corners of Utah, Arizona, and New Mexico. A day's ride on horseback from Durango brings the traveler into the midst of these prehistoric relics. In an area of 6,000 square miles examined by the United States Geological Survey, there is scarcely a square mile that does not furnish evidence of previous occupation by a race totally distinct from the nomadic savages who hold it now, and in many ways greatly superior to them. Of the strange people who once occupied these narrow valleys, and built their fortress dwellings far up in the almost inaccessible cliffs history is silent. From whence they came, in what manner they acquired their architectural skill, and by what calamities they perished from the face of the earth, are secrets yet to be discovered.

The ruins nearest Durango, including many of the most important yet found, are located on the Rio Mancos, Rio de la Plata, Rio San Juan, and in Montezuma, Hovenweep and McElmo Cañons. They may be classified as lowland or agricultural settlements, cave dwellings, and cliff houses, or fortresses. The cliff houses could only have been used as places of refuge or defense. All these ruins are built of stone, generally smoothly hewn, and laid with the skill of the best modern mason. Some are in the shape of parallelograms, and others are circular in form, the squares being perfect squares and the circles perfect circles. Most of the buildings are rectangular, but connected with many are large circular towers, frequently as much as forty feet in diameter, and in some cases having triple walls. They are solidly built of hewn stone, dressed on the outside to the curve, neatly jointed, and laid in mortar.

The country may be described as a great mesa, or table-land, through which the streams have cut deep cañons, the sides of which are high cliffs of perpendicular rocks. Far up the face of these cliffs, often several hundred feet above the valley, usually in natural recesses or alcoves, are the cliff houses, or fortresses, reached only by ladders, or steps cut into the rock, with small holes for the hands. They appear in all sorts of unexpected places; the walls frequently extending from the ledge below to the overhanging rocks in such a manner as to be hardly distinguishable at a little distance. Some of the highest and most difficult of access, and on that account the most notable and interesting, have been discovered only after a

CLIFF DWELLINGS, MANCOS CAÑON.

close examination of the cliffs with a powerful field glass. In describing some of these, situated on the Rio Mancos, Mr. W. H. Holmes, of the United States Geological Survey, who visited this section in 1875–6, says:

"So cleverly are these houses hidden away in the dark recesses, and so very like the surrounding cliffs in color, that I had almost completed the sketch of the upper house before the lower, or 'sixteen windowed,' one was detected. They are at least 800 hundred feet above the river. The lower 500 hundred feet is of rough cliff-broken slope, the remainder of massive, bedded sandstone, full of wind-worn niches, crevices and caves. Within 100 feet of the cliff-top, set deep in a great niche, with arched, overhanging roof, is the upper house, its front wall built along the very brink of a sheer precipice. Thirty feet below, in a similar but less remarkable niche, is the larger house, with its long line of apertures, which I afterward found to be openings intended rather for the insertion of beams than for windows."

Mr. W. H. Jackson, of Denver, photographer of the Hayden survey, who has made the most comprehensive reports upon these ruins, thus alludes to the Pueblo of Chettro Kettle, in Chaco Cañon, within the borders of New Mexico: "In this ruin there was at one time a line of wall running around three sides of the building 935 feet in length and about 40 feet in height, giving 37,400 square feet of surface, and as an average of 50 pieces of stone appeared within the space of every square foot, this would give nearly 2,000,000 pieces for the surface of the outer wall alone; multiply this by the opposite surface, and also by the interior and transverse lines of masonry, and, supposing a symmetrical terracing, we find that it will swell the total up into more than 30,000,000, embraced within about 315,000 cubic feet of masonry. These millions of pieces had to be quarried, dressed roughly to fit their places, and carefully adapted to it; the massive timbers had to be brought from a considerable distance, cut and fitted to their places in the wall, and covered with other courses; and then the other details of window and roof making, plastering, and construction of ladders, must have employed a large body of intelligent, well organized, patient and industrious people, under thorough discipline, for a very long time."

HEALTH.

It is a remarkable fact that a large proportion, probably nearly one-half, of all the people now residing in Colorado were influenced in coming here, either directly or indirectly, by considerations of health. Of these many came for well defined reasons; as in the case of asthmatics, to whom the climate offers an almost infallible specific; and consumptives, who frequently mend here with astonishing rapidity. Others accompanied relatives or friends who were in ill health, and because there was at least a possibility of benefit in a change of climate. "My wife cannot live at the East." "My husband never enjoyed good health till he came to Colorado." Such are the remarks heard daily wherever people meet for social intercourse.

That so much should be said and written in regard to the climate is not singular, for, whatever its merits or demerits, it possesses a distinctive character, very different from that of any of the states east of the Missouri river. This is due principally to the difference in altitude. Very little of the habitable portion of the state lies at a less elevation than one mile above the level of the sea, and some of the mining towns are situated at twice that height; which fact, modified by certain peculiarities of the contour of the country and its soil, gives rise to three notable conditions that affect its healthfulness. First of these we may mention the rarefaction of the air, which has only about four-fifths of the density at Denver that it possesses at sea level. This is humorously put forward to account for everything unusual that may be noted, for which the "light air" is a convenient scapegoat. It exacts a tribute of recognition from nearly all who enter the state, for even at Colorado Springs or Denver there are few "tenderfeet" who care to run up stairs upon their first arrival, while at Leadville and Kokomo even a leisurely walk overtaxes both heart and lungs. The newcomer is apt to be afflicted with an indefinable nervousness, sometimes amounting to positive distress, which may be traced to this cause. But gradually the lungs expand and become accustomed to the new order of things, so that in most instances no further inconvenience is felt. Second in importance is the dryness of the atmosphere, and the consequent infrequency of cloudy weather and storms. With many people sunshine is considered the *sine qua non* of cheerfulness and health; in Colorado we find the maximum of clear days. Colorado people returning East for a few weeks' visit, seldom fail on getting back to berate the climate of the "States," and to declare that life without sunshine is little better than vegetation. The number of clear days in a year, at Denver, as shown by the Signal Service reports, is 302. The number of days when the sun cannot be seen at all, or its location distinguished through the clouds, is expressed by zero. "Old Sol" is a stand-by in Colorado, and a genuinely cloudy day, as known at the East, where the clouds show no trace of his presence, but shut down like an impenetrable pall, is as rare as a total eclipse. Third, we may add, a cool atmosphere; for although the temperature is sometimes raised very high by the noonday sun in summer, it is seldom too warm in the shade, and at nightfall there is usually a quick cooling of the air that increases until daybreak. This is occasioned by the fact that the dry air does not hold the heat as moist air would. The average winter temperature is rather lower than that of other localities of the same latitude at a less elevation, but it is apparently warmer, owing to the excess of sunshine, and the absence of moisture.

These conditions are all favorable to an active, out-of-door life, and few of those whose ailments will allow them to lead such a life fail to find a tonic in the pure air of the plains and mountains. Here is plenty of space for a free, untrammeled existence,—for here are only 200,000 people in a state as large as all New England, New York and New Jersey combined. Other considerations not connected with the climate are worth mentioning. This is a new community, in which conservatism is little esteemed and stagnation is impossible. Those who did not come here for their health came here to make money,—not infrequently to retrieve past reverses. New plans, new hopes, new enterprises, new prospects, new possibilities, are the entrancing themes that meet one at every turn. The new-comer starts a new business in a new building, in a new quarter, among new neighbors, who are as newly arrived as himself; sends his children to a new school in a new schoolhouse and goes to hear a new preacher in a new church. Every morning he reads of a new mining excitement in a new part of the state, new strikes in old mines, and probably an elaborate account of a newly projected railway whose managers seem to consider the building of five or six hundred miles of track through the mountains to some new mining district a mere trifle.

Thin-blooded dyspeptics, those afflicted with scrofula, those worn down with malarial diseases, those suffering from mental depression and nervous exhaustion, those predisposed to consumption or possessing weak lungs, those already advanced in consumption, if not too far gone, which should be decided by a competent physician, and nearly all who are scourged with asthma, together with a vast number who suffer from general debility and lack of stamina, induced by the over-work that is killing so many Americans, may come to Colorado with benefit to their health in the majority of cases. Rheumatism and catarrh are seldom aggravated, and in occasional instances may be relieved, by the Colorado climate.

The average percentage of saturation of the air with vapor at Denver and Colorado Springs, as compared with stations on the Atlantic coast, is forty-six per cent for the former to seventy per cent for the latter. There is, especially during the fall and winter, a remarkable development of atmospheric electricity, which is conceded to be the best of tonics to those enfeebled by sickness. The effect of elevation upon atmospheric germs is thought to be antagonistic, and it is certain that they are less obnoxious in a dry, cool air.

Here, then, we may recapitulate some of the inducements offered by Colorado to invalids: A cool, dry, bracing atmosphere, kept in motion by frequent winds, and highly charged with electricity; a dry, gravelly soil, that is a natural foe to malaria; and an unusual number of bright, sunny days, when it is natural to seek out-door exercise. To these are added scenic attractions which are often strong enough to enable the invalid to forget his ailments in the engrossing occupation of exploring the mountains and parks, till perchance he finds his health restored before he is willing to admit the fact, and return again to the sober routine of labor.

When we come to treat of particular portions of Colorado and northern New Mexico adapted for health resorts, their name is legion. Denver, Colorado Springs, and Manitou, the latter ranking first, are especially suitable for ladies. Elegant and attractive hotels and boarding houses, fine walks, rides and drives, medicinal waters, fashionable amusements, and refined society, are combined to place them on a level with the noted eastern watering-places; while the grandeur of Pike's Peak and Cheyenne Mountain, the sublime depths of the cañons, and the majesty of the great plains, are features all our own.

Those who want a succession of new sensations and a spice of romance can camp out on the plains, and study the life of the sheep herders and cow-boys, lie in wait for the wary antelope, or loose the greyhound and watch his pursuit of the fleet jack-rabbits; or lose themselves in the solitude of the mountain gorges, amidst the haunts of the cinnamon bear and mountain lion.

Camping excursions, with wagons and tents, into the parks are very popular. Frequently the whole family goes for a month or more, and partakes of a taste of Arcadia, to come back again sunbrowned and dust-begrimed, but healthy and happy, with a store of anecdotes and reminiscences to last a year.

The more prominent health resorts and medicinal waters will be found treated of in the consecutive descriptions of localities along the different divisions of the Denver & Rio Grande Railway.

SPORT.

A FINE sporting country lies contiguous to the Denver & Rio Grande Railway, along the entire extent of its mountain divisions. The principal varieties of game found are deer, antelope, elk, bear, wild turkey, quail, sage hens, wild geese and ducks. Occasionally a fortunate hunter gets a shot at a mountain sheep (in the Elk Mountains they are quite common), and more frequently a mountain lion is slain, and his hide added to the collection of some museum. Everywhere the mountain streams abound with speckled trout, holding out prime temptations to the angler. With many the rarest of sport is enjoyed in chasing antelope or rabbits upon the plains with hounds. Nowhere else in America are greyhounds so numerous as here, and they seem, by the law of the survival of the fittest, likely to still further increase.

In the San Luis Park, between Alamosa and Saguache, are the San Luis lakes, or marshes, in which may be found a profusion of wild geese and ducks. These marshes are reached by a day's drive from Alamosa, and are readily traversed on foot. Swans, also, are found there, and white brant, or snow geese, as well as sand-hill cranes.

On the mountains, between Antonito and Durango, near Los Pinos creek and the Chama river, are extensive regions almost devoid of settlements, and heretofore seldom reached by sportsmen. Here are broad plateaus and pleasant valleys, where game is abundant, the climate unsurpassed, and nothing wanting that the hunter can desire. To camp out among the pines and stalk deer and elk, untroubled by mosquitoes or flies, with venison and trout for diet, plenty of elbow-room, and scenery that might entrance the soul, is a consummation any sportsman might covet.

All the San Juan region abounds in game, and the streams and lakes are full of trout. Durango, Silverton, Lake City, Ouray, are all excellent head-quarters for the hunter, and he will have no difficulty in soon discovering plenty of elk and deer, and if so disposed a grizzly or a cinnamon bear.

To the northward, in the Elk Mountain country, near the Gunnison Division, game is equally abundant. Elk were so numerous during the past winter that hundreds of those noble animals were slaughtered out of mere wantonness,—or rather pure wickedness. Beyond the Saguache range, near Red Cliff, are also favorite ranges for game of all kinds found in the state.

A small party starting out with saddle-horses and pack-mules, and carrying their tents with them, can always find good hunting, uncommonly free from the drawbacks of heat, insects, mud, and bad weather, that torture the huntsman in less elevated regions.

ALTITUDES.

The following table shows the elevation in feet above the level of the sea of the localities named.

Alamosa	7,492	Mountain of the Holy Cross	14,176
Alpine Pass	11,525	Mount Elbert	14,351
Animas City	6,622	Mount Evans	14,330
Animas Forks	11,200	Mount Harvard	14,375
Antelope Park	9,000	Mount Massive	14,368
Antonito	7,833	Mount Rosalie	14,340
Aspen	7,775	Mount Shavano	14,239
Blaine's Peak	13,905	Mount Sneffels	14,158
Buena Vista	7,874	Mount Wilson	14,280
Cañon City	5,287	Mount Yale	14,187
Castle Peak	14,115	Mouth of Rio Navajo	6,340
Castle Rock	6,180	Mouth of Rio Piedras	6,030
Cochetopa Pass	10,057	Mule Shoe Curve	8,725
Colorado Springs	5,947	Ojo Caliente	6,000
Conejos	7,880	Ouray	7,640
Continental Divide, San Juan Division	7,500	Pagosa Springs	7,108
		Pike's Peak	14,147
Cottonwood Springs	7,950	Pinos-Chama Summit	9,552
Cuchara	5,866	Poncho Pass	8,931
Culebra Mountain	14,069	Poncho Springs	7,350
Cumbres	9,962	Pridgeon's Peak	14,054
Del Norte	7,750	Pueblo	4,713
Denver	5,197	Pyramid Peak	14,146
Divide	7,186	Red Cliff	8,470
Durango	6,545	Robinson	10,781
El Moro	5,825	Rosita	8,500
Engineer Mountain	13,076	Ruby Camp	10,500
Fort Garland	7,882	Saguache	7,723
Fremont Pass	11,540	San Luis Lakes	7,592
Grand Cañon of the Arkansas, east end	5,416	San Luis Peak	14,100
		Sierra Blanca	14,464
Grand Cañon of the Arkansas, west end	5,639	Silver Cliff	7,816
		Silverton	9,780
Granite	8,831	Simpson's Peak	14,055
Gunnison City	7,743	Snow Mass Mountain	13,970
Handie's Peak	14,149	Spanish Peaks { West	13,620
Howardsville	9,700	Spanish Peaks { East	12,720
Hunt's Peak	14,056	Stewart's Peak	14,032
Irwin	10,500	South Arkansas	6,900
Kokomo	10,408	Tennessee Park	9,877
Lake City	8,550	Tennessee Pass	10,334
La Veta	6,970	Teocalli Mountain	13,113
Leadville	10,139	Toltec Station	9,411
Long's Peak	14,271	Twin Lakes	9,357
Los Pinos	8,968	Uncompahgre Peak	14,235
Malta	9,613	Veta Mountain	14,176
Manitou	6,297	Veta Pass	9,339
Maroon Mountain	14,003	Westcliffe	7,700
Marshall Pass	10,725	Wetterhorn Mountain	14,069
Mount Antero	14,245		

CONDENSED MAP

OF THE

DENVER & RIO GRANDE RAILWAY.

THE SCENIC LINE OF AMERICA.

PULLMAN PALACE SLEEPERS, HORTON RECLINING-CHAIR COACHES, MODEL OPEN OBSERVATION CARS.

WESTINGHOUSE AIR BRAKES, MILLER COUPLERS, STEEL RAILS, IRON BRIDGES, ROCK BALLAST.

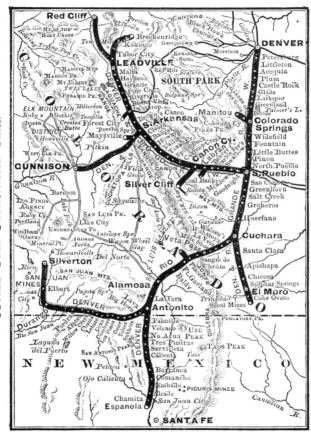